AWAKENING
ON THE
ROAD

BOOK I THE EAST

*The Story of My Travels around the World and My
Discovery of the Invisible Forces of the Universe*

F I L I P   Z I O L K O W S K I

BALBOA.
PRESS

A DIVISION OF HAY HOUSE

Balboa Press books may be ordered through booksellers or by contacting:

Balboa Press
A Division of Hay House
1663 Liberty Drive
Bloomington, IN 47403
www.balboapress.com
1 (877) 407-4847

Because of the dynamic nature of the Internet, any web addresses or links contained in this book may have changed since publication and may no longer be valid. The views expressed in this work are solely those of the author and do not necessarily reflect the views of the publisher, and the publisher hereby disclaims any responsibility for them.

The author of this book does not dispense medical advice or prescribe the use of any technique as a form of treatment for physical, emotional, or medical problems without the advice of a physician, either directly or indirectly. The intent of the author is only to offer information of a general nature to help you in your quest for emotional and spiritual well-being. In the event you use any of the information in this book for yourself, which is your constitutional right, the author and the publisher assume no responsibility for your actions.

Any people depicted in stock imagery provided by Thinkstock are models, and such images are being used for illustrative purposes only. Certain stock imagery © Thinkstock.

Printed in the United States of America.

ISBN: 978-1-4525-1870-1 (sc)
ISBN: 978-1-4525-1872-5 (hc)
ISBN: 978-1-4525-1871-8 (e)

Library of Congress Control Number: 2014912751

Balboa Press rev. date: 8/20/2014

Dedicated to

My loving parents
Iwona and Wladyslaw

"The journey of a thousands miles begins with the first step"

Lao Tzu

Contents

Foreword

Filip's journey is a universal experience. In life, we all seek to find our identity, to enjoy meaningful love and to contribute to life through inspiring work that is our passion. These were all his big picture goals when he set out to see the world.

The difference is in the way he crafted his travels and followed the inspiration he felt from a very early age. His dream to freely travel was born out of an un-free upbringing in Communist Poland. It makes his journey all the more inspiring when you consider the courage and strength it took for him to follow that dream. It is an amazing journey made all the more amazing because we get to see the world through his eyes and get a glimpse into the influences in his upbringing that came to bear in the adventures he encountered.

He very clearly expresses his unique focus in this passage from his book:

"For me, a key part of any trip was the people I met and the connections I built with them. Of course I wanted to visit the highlights of each place, walk the city streets, swim in the oceans and trek the mountains but what I wanted more was to explore new cultures and meet the locals and other traveling free spirits. I was thirsty for long conversations about life, the Universe and understanding global issues from different perspectives."

Filip couldn't tell you as much about the sites he saw as he could about every detail of the people he encountered. It is almost as if he wrote this book as a *people-logue* instead of a *travelogue*.

"Awakening on the Road" is an epic journey that winds its way around the world, first in the East and then in the West. It is inspired by a desire to experience more about life and understand nature of human reality. It joins an incredible counter-culture of worldwide backpackers who meet each other, connect for a while, collect contact information, go off on individual adventures, and then either by design or chance, find each other again in some other country or city.

At only 38 years old, he has already accomplished what most of us would take two lifetimes to do. His journeys in the East were only the tip of the iceberg of his discoveries. The fulfillment of his goals to find himself, bring a message of love, compassion and peace to the world as he traveled through it, his desire to meet people and to fall in love began in the East and came to full maturity and flow during his journeys in the West. There was so much to tell that his quest filled two books.

Through challenging adventures, Filip eventually discovers a place where he begins to see his role in the whole of human evolution. His awakening process is sometimes frustrating, sometimes breathtaking, sometimes scary but always honest. In the end, he puts the pieces of his explorations into perspective with the greatest outcome of joy and victory over the questions.

Inspiring journey!

Preface

This book is the result of a deep desire to share my travel experiences and the spiritual awakening they birthed. The journey began in my teenage years when I set the simplest yet most challenging goal possible for myself:

To travel around the world

I personally did not know anyone who had done such a thing before nor did I know how I would do it but I intuitively trusted that my goal would be fulfilled somehow.

Fifteen years later in 2007, I left a lucrative corporate IT job in London, England and bought a one-way ticket to Pisa, Italy. This was my first trip of the Eastern half of my around the world tour. It ended with a breathtaking experience in the Himalayas. Ultimately, my journeys after Asia included travels to the West. The whole excursion lasted more than two and a half years and ended up in Cali, Colombia where I have lived for the past four years.

Making the courageous decision to step out of my secure life and explore the world delivered the most unexpected, empowering and luminous transformation. I found my purpose, came to understand how the Law of Attraction played out in my travel adventures and discovered the magic of the unseen forces that guided my explorations.

Today living in Cali, I am a professor who teaches courses in marketing, advertising and design at the University in Cali. Spiritually, my life has opened to my personal power and potential beyond anything I could have imagined.

I invite you to read about my journey in the stories I have shared here; consider the Awakening Insights that were important personal teachings in my discovery process that I would like to pass along to you; and decide for yourself if traveling to distant lands is part of your path of transformation as it was mine. If it is, then do it.

I hope you will find my experiences interesting. Perhaps they will inspire you to explore who you are and find what you want from your own life. Maybe along the way you will encounter your own invisible forces and learn as I did that we are all deeply connected and that ...*we are far more powerful, capable of peace and wired for love than we ever imagined!*

Acknowledgments

The book would not come into this world if not for the persistence of Virginia Morrel from Balboa Press. Her charm, soft selling skills and kindness motivated me to complete the book. Thank you to Kellie Poulin for using her amazing editorial skills to make this book into a great story. Without her help, this story would never sound as good as it does. Gratitude goes to Przemek Rochon, Michael Place and other travelers who put pressure on me to start and finish this work.

And a special thank you to Juanita for being my inspiration.

"Awakening on the Road" is also the result of the encouragement that I received from various friends I met throughout the world. They gave me insights about improving the manuscript and making it the best story ever. To those people I say, "Thank you for trusting in me! Without you I would not have completed it."

Special thanks to

Iwona i Wladyslaw Ziolkowscy, Maciej Ziolkowski, Zofia Ziolkowska, Juanita Peña, Michal Lange, Ash, Kuba, Wujek Wlodek, Cielo, Darius Slusarczyk, Urs Diethel, Niklas Richardson, Allen Manning, Anney Wyner, Robert Matson, Peter Wilson, Minos Makris, Stevie Halls, Gladys Ella, Przemyslaw Rochon, Santana, Michael Place, Maria Fernanda Camacho, Mario Uribe, Alvaro Rojas, Monica Piedrahita, Bartek Piasecki, Maggie Robbinson, David Valencia, Piotr Kszysztof, Filippo Malvezzi, Kinga Knapinska, Manuel Saldarriaga, Pasikonik, Szymon Kochanski, Bobby Mc Man, Jona de Beuck, Jeson Seward, Ally Butterworth, Fernando Pechs, Aldona Kmiec, Maria Moreno, Magdalena Fraczek, Ewa Trzaskalska, Ilan Sternberg, Carolina Ramon Tovar, Bartlomiej Luszcz, Tomasz Pietrukaniec, Dariusz Szorc, Bartosz Zbroja, Ewelina Rosiek, Arkadiusz Jazdzejewski, Pietro Messa, Marcin Kowalczyk, Wayne Mondesir, Piotr Kowalski, Kaz Westen, Carolina Libertad, Tomek Braszka, Pauline Rafal, Diego Espindola, Johanna Pino Provoste, Piotr Staron, Kai Zhao, Malgorzata Olszanowska, Greg A. Ebersole, Delana Thompson, Kai Zhao, Bart Pogoda, Nikki Hignett, Taita Floro Agrega and all the wonderful people who have influenced my life.

Introduction

He who travels changes...

Let me introduce myself. My name is Filip and I am a soul traveler on the road of life.

In June 2000, I left the security of my comfort zone by traveling from my native Poland to work part-time for a small advertising agency in New York City. A few years later, I moved to the UK to further establish my professional credentials. After three years of employment as a web design manager in central London, I had saved enough to begin my long awaited trip around the world.

I was more than ready to find out about the realities of life that I intuitively felt awaited me on the road. While I knew it would be exciting, I could never have predicted that it would be such a life-changing experience.

Initially I thought about leaving for a year and then coming back to continue my career. However, when I discovered the absolute joy of traveling and the sense of aliveness I experienced, I was unable to stop. Then the travel wasn't just an extended vacation or a 'gap' year for me. This was an intentional life choice. My work and profession became that of traveler.

It didn't take long for me to see that I had made one of the best decisions in my life. As a result of that realization, I ended up exploring the world for two and a half years. I 'adventured' my way through more than fifty countries on four continents before finally settling down in Cali, Colombia in January 2010. This book is the story of the first year of those adventures that ends with my extraordinary trek in the Himalayas.

During my trip I lost cameras, laptops, I-Pods, as well as a video camera. I was exposed to enormous human kindness and some life threatening, unpleasant situations. I spent almost all of my savings but my web design skills allowed me to work remotely, which gave me peace and a sense of monetary independence.

This is my unique journey as an explorer of Eastern Europe and Asia. While the tourist attractions and points of interest were defining directions of my itinerary, I realized that I was more inclined to observe and spend time in conversation with the locals getting to know them, their lifestyle, culture and beliefs. As a result, this book reflects both the traveler's point of view and my personal interactive perspectives.

Writing this book helped me connect the dots of my spiritual journey that evolved as a consequence of the travel decisions I made, the people I met and the powerful moments I was privileged to experience.

The content is fully based on real stories, real people and pleasant and painful lessons that I learned on the road. Some of the names in the book have been changed in order to protect peoples' privacy.

This book is organized into five parts:

> Part I gives information about my background.
> Part II describes the discovery process of the influences in my life that led me to take on the identity of 'explorer' and world traveler.
> Part III describes the small weekend trips I took to test my future 'traveler' status.
> Part IV, "On the Road", is the story of my journey through various countries and continents and
> Part V reveals my learning from all that I experienced in the first year of my world exploration.

Feel free to choose to read what is of interest to you. If you are looking to find out about the invisible forces of the universe and the inspiration I was exposed to, I recommend you read the story from the beginning. But if you are only interested in the travel part, feel free to jump right into Parts III and IV where you will find many travel stories and insights. If your goal is to read about deep spiritual reality you will find it mostly in Part IV about India and in Part V that reflects upon my personal evolutionary process and the rewards and challenges of traveling solo.

No matter how much you read or where you start, I hope you will find useful tips on how to travel on your own, maybe discover your passion and perhaps as a result of reading my book be inspired to one day hit the road to find your purpose through travel as I did.

For some, this book might serve as an inspiration and for others it may be a revelation of the complex world in which we live. I hope even the most dismissive readers will find some of the stories fascinating, thrilling or evocative enough to open their minds to discovering something new and constructive for themselves.

The purpose of this book is to show you that everything is possible if you have a big enough dream and you follow your passion.

Important note

All comments, generalizations, traveling and awakening insights included in this book are based solely on my own experience and should not be taken as absolute truth. The intention here is to inspire and light the spark of adventure in those who wish for more in their lives.

PART I

SOWING THE SEEDS OF THE JOURNEY

My First Deep Spiritual Experience

I stared out the window of the bus as the scenery passed by in a blur. I was lost in thought about my life and the many questions that consumed my attention - questions with no answers.

My fellow Christian summer camp attendees and I were being transported the two hundred miles from our wilderness base into my hometown, Gdansk to explore a famous cathedral in Oliwa, the old district of the city. As the bus made its way to Gdansk, I had plenty of time to ponder my history so far in my short 15 years on earth:

...I was born in 1976 in Gdansk, Poland and raised in a middle class, Catholic Polish family. Religion was a powerful influence in our culture and in my life.

As a young teenager, even though I was religious as were my friends, I was often filled with questions about the lack of logic in what I had been taught about God and Jesus and what I heard from the priests in my church. For me, my life was always about seeking the truth and it seemed in short supply at the moment:

The questions kept rolling through my young mind: Does God really exist? What does he look like? Why is there so much injustice in the world? What happened to Jesus when he was fifteen, twenty, twenty-five years old? What happened to Mary? How can we prove that she was pregnant without having had sex with Joseph? Why is the Bible so complicated?

My mind floated back to the conversation I had shared with the Bible Camp team leader the night before. Throughout my stay at this summer camp, I had struggled with the Bible

3

teachings that were in conflict with my Catholic upbringing. There was some deep disturbance inside me about what I was hearing that caused me to rebel and doubt everything I had been told.

"Filip, I know where you are coming from. All I can say is, if you are in doubt, pray to God for a sign." The team leader's eyes had been alight with fervent belief.

"Do you mean that I have to pray to God to see if what you teach is the truth?" I had asked.

"We do not teach, we only pass on the words of Jesus." He had matter-of-factly informed me.

"But it doesn't make sense for me to believe that Jesus died for our sins in order to save us *all* from hell when there are good people in the world who do not believe in that story or who have never heard of Jesus. Are you saying they won't be saved? I find so many contradictions in the Bible and the teachings of Jesus that I don't know what to trust is true. I guess it depends on the interpretation of each person." I had protested, doubtful and confused.

"There is no interpretation. You will receive all the answers soon. First you must pray for a sign as I did." His voice had been filled with unshakeable confidence.

That night, I did what he had advised. I took their Bible in hand and I prayed for a sign. The next day I was told we were going for a day trip to Gdansk, to visit a famous church. This church was known for its beautiful Baroque organ inlaid with marble. When it was played, it was said that the carved figures of trumpeting angels that adorned its structure would begin to move in synchronization with the music.

...I was jolted out of my reflections as the bus came to a stop outside the church and I moved with the rest of my group into the cathedral.

As I entered through the doors, it was as if I stepped back in time to the innocence of my childhood when going to church was a simple act of praying to God without questioning

4

anything. The beautiful sound of the organ music filled the space and vibrated through my entire body. I sat down in the middle row of pews and noticed that, although the music was being played, none of the famous sculptures were moving as I had heard they were supposed to be when the music played. I wanted to be shown something of the truth about presence of God and Jesus. The advice of the team leader came to me so I began to pray for a sign.

I slid into deep prayer and sincerely asked God to move the figures. I had barely finished with my request when I heard the scraping sound of moving objects. I looked up and saw that the whole lot of trumpeting angels started moving in rhythm to the music. In that moment I knew it was a sign from God. I felt completely in awe of what was occurring before me. My heart was filled with the wonder of the magic I was witnessing. There was no doubt about what I was seeing. Then, as suddenly as it began, the movement of the angels stopped.

I closed my eyes, bowed my head and prayed to God again.

"God I know it is unfair to ask twice for a sign, but please forgive me for being a Doubting Thomas. If it was really a sign from you, please move the angels again as you just did. If you do I will spread your word from the Bible to all my friends and will accept Jesus as my salvation." I promised.

As soon as I stopped praying, the incredibly loud sound filled the cathedral space again. When I raised my head, I saw the angels starting to move and shake as they came alive for a second time.

I felt tears of gratitude and joy streaming down my cheeks. I knew in my heart that I had experienced a deep truth about forces that were beyond my physical ability to see. I somehow knew I could call on this powerful presence to be a part of my life always...it was the seed that began my life journey to know more...

My Early Years

Poland was a country that was politically controlled by the Soviet Union yet enjoyed a less oppressive version of Communism. I grew up there in a very traditional, middle-class, Polish household where my father was the patriarch of our family and my mother, in addition to working outside the home, was the teacher, nurturer and the loving presence in our lives.

My father worked in West Germany to support our family of four, which included himself, my mom, my brother and me. His income provided us with some rare Western World luxuries. In fact, I was the only one in the neighborhood who had such enviable toys as Matchbox mini cars, Legos, an Atari XL and later, an Amiga 500.

My mother tried to sow the seeds of inspiration and a passion for learning in my brother and me. I was one of a few fortunate children who already knew the basics of mathematics, language, history of the world, geography, biology, anthropology and even astronomy by the time I started my formal education. That is why the first years of primary school were easy for me and I excelled in my studies.

Not only was I well educated in my early years I was also mentally trained to compete and win. My older cousin, my uncle and my grandmother encouraged me to improve myself both intellectually and physically. My cousins and I were constantly challenging one another in various sports events, which developed a fierce desire in me to win. Losing was never my strength.

I grew up loving the music of Depeche Mode, composing electronic music on my Amiga computer, practicing judo and playing football.

When I was 12, my father took me to Germany for my first 'out of country' adventure. The rest of my family was a bit skeptical about this excursion because I was so young and because Germany was such an expensive place to visit. Nonetheless, that two-week experience completely changed my perception of the world.

For the first time I saw bright colors in the streets, discovered ice cream with more than three flavors and witnessed firsthand all the models of cars I had only seen in the pirated VHS movies at my neighbor's weekend video sessions. I remember other firsts as well: the sweet taste of Coca Cola and the excitement of a roller coaster ride at the Dinosaur Luna Park in Düsseldorf.

After that trip with my father, I knew I wanted to explore the world to see what else was out there.

The Influence Of Books

When I was 14, the political system in the whole of Eastern Europe changed and I was exposed to the early phase of wild capitalism in my home country. It was a time that gave us all a sense of freedom and joy. We had access to Western products, were able to procure passports and saw new opportunities open up for us.

I was raised in the shadow of the ambitious standards of the Western world and it taught me to compete with others and to see winning as the only way to feel successful. My upbringing neither prepared me for opening to the deeper question of who I am nor did it help me find my purpose in life. It took more than thirty years for that to happen and for me to comprehend the power of human emotions and discern what was truly important.

My first introduction to the path of personal growth began when I was 17 years old with a chance meeting of a co-worker of my mom's who recommended the book "Awakening the Giant Within" by Anthony Robbins. When I read it, I was instantly inspired to be all I could be. For me, that meant becoming a famous Polish rock star. I soon stopped my other activities to take up rock music.

I learned to sing, play guitar and even composed catchy pop rock songs. Before the grunge music scene made its way from Seattle to Poland, I was a huge Guns'n'Roses fan. I grew my hair and a little mustache and waited patiently for a beard to follow. (It took me a while!)

I was so inspired by the Anthony Robbins book, that I started to search for similar topics at the local esoteric bookstore.

I found a book entitled, "How to Get Control of Your Time and Your Life" written in 1973 by Alan Lakein where the author shared his experience and expertise on how to be productive. I was keen on reaching my goals as quickly as possible so this information was invaluable to me.

AWAKENING INSIGHT
*If you knew you could achieve anything
in your life what would you do?*

One of the chapters spoke about the power of inspiring questions. One of the questions that caught my full attention was: *If you knew you could achieve anything in your life what would you do?*

As instructed, I wrote down everything that came to mind. It suggested that the exercise include such diverse items as exploring my sexuality and traveling the world. My list was extensive given my interests at the time. I wanted to finish university with good grades, find a beautiful girlfriend, have a good job, to become a famous rock musician and so on. These were nice ideas and all quite possible to achieve but I did not feel *inspired* by them.

I read the chapter again and when I put all my attention on the words *"if you knew you could achieve anything"* I suddenly realized that, for me, nothing was more inspiring and more seemingly impossible than Lakein's suggestion of traveling around the world. No one I knew had ventured farther than Germany, our neighboring country. It was clear to me that exploring the entire planet was the biggest dream one could dare to dream. The spark of inspiration had been ignited. I knew that any future life choices I made had to be based on this *passion* rather than the promise of money or the lure of a successful career.

With my chosen goal of traveling around the world, I turned back to study the advice of Anthony Robbins as a way to make it a reality. Robbins suggested that I find a way to take small action steps toward a goal. I went to the local bookstore and bought a world map as my first small baby step. I put it on my wall and thought about places worth visiting. The world was huge and I had no idea where to start.

AWAKENING INSIGHT
Even a small action shows the Universe that you are serious and passionate about your goals.

Using pictures in a photo album taken from my mother's bookshelf, I pinned the sites on the map that attracted me. There were exotic and magical places around the world such as Stonehenge, the Pyramids of Egypt and Machu Picchu in Peru that caught my eye. It was a simple act to hang the map and pin the pictures of these interesting places. Every night before going to sleep and every morning as I woke up, I would look at locations and imagine what it would be like to actually go there. Each time I looked at the 'world on my wall' and thought about it, I was programming my subconscious toward making my dream a reality.

Sixteen years later, I was on a thirty month, epic journey around the world. It started in the East, finished in the West and took me through more than fifty countries on four continents.

PART II

CONNECTING THE DOTS

1991-2006

"You can't connect the dots looking forward; you can only connect them looking backwards. So you have to trust that the dots will somehow connect in your future. You have to trust in something — your gut, destiny, life, karma, whatever. This approach has never let me down, and it has made all the difference in my life."
~ Steve Jobs

Understanding life and unfolding your personal journey often requires the perspective of time and the ability to look back at the perfection of every life detail that contributed to first, *realizing* and then, *fulfilling* your dream.

It was no different for me...

In writing this book, I became fully aware of many events in my early life that were simply building my ability and preparing me for my traveling adventures and the personal growth side effects of such a life-altering trek.

From my early spiritual experiences to my education to my passionate pursuit of music, I recognized a deeper wisdom at work in me. Connecting the dots of my pre-travel life painted a surprising picture of my soul's voice. It became crystal clear that I was destined to explore the world and was guided by the unseen hand of the Universe to discover the purpose and meaning of my life through my travel adventures.

AWAKENING INSIGHT
If you take the time to consider your choices, experiences and strengths, you can connect the dots of your personal journey and find your unique soul-guided path.

First Dot

Prayer And The Early Steps Of My Spirituality

My spiritual journey started when I was very young. Even though my parents were not regular church-going people, they did their best to raise my brother and I in the Catholic tradition, which was quite common in Poland. In their own way, both my parents taught me about respecting God and the Bible.

My father would take us to church at Christmas and Easter, which was always special. I loved the reverent silence and the mantra-like repetition and chanting of group prayers. The smell of incense and the warm glow that emanated from the candles gave me a sense of sacred comfort. In church, I felt God's presence but I took a rather respectful, somewhat fearful approach to him as one would to a father. In my life, He was always available if I was in need but He never felt very close in the sense of being loving friend.

My father was quite a happy man, despite his challenging upbringing of growing up without a father. He had to learn how to survive and embrace his traditional male role at an early age. He discovered that he had to work hard, be strong and that, in order to feel safe, he had to make the right decisions on his own. His independence made him cautious in his trust of people and there was little room for love or spirituality in his life. Understandably, he had no idea about the concept of the Universe at work in his life.

His favorite saying was, "Do unto others as you would have them do unto you." He also admitted that he never understood the teachings of Jesus from the Bible that spoke about loving your enemies and turning the other cheek.

My mother, on the other hand, often quoted Jesus' instruction to "Love others as you love yourself." As early as I can remember, she was always interested in understanding spirituality and the mysteries of life.

I learned about prayer from her and my grandmother. They taught me that praying involved first a simple but sincere greeting to Father God or Mother Mary followed by a continual repetition of the request.

It came in handy when my parents would fight. I remember my brother and I getting down on our knees and praying to God for help in the way we had learned. It seemed our prayers were answered because soon after we prayed, they stopped their loud disagreements and quiet was restored to our home. As a result of these outcomes, I saw prayer as an effective problem solver.

AWAKENING INSIGHT
Prayer is an effective and powerful
way to solve most problems.

Even though I was quite religious in my teen years, I struggled to find peace at church and to understand the truth about the existence and identity of God. My questions never felt like they were answered to my satisfaction until my miraculous and magical experience in the cathedral in Gdansk. When I saw the immediate result of my prayers, I was overjoyed and completely believed I had found the answers I had been seeking.

When I returned home after Bible Camp and my glorious 'God experience' in the church, I had only one mission: to spread the message in the Bible and convince everyone that

Jesus is the only salvation. I fervently believed that in order to reach heaven and avoid hell, one had to admit to being a sinner, take Jesus into their hearts and accept Him as their Savior. I was a bit surprised that most of my friends saw my fervor more as craziness and brainwashing than a religious mission.

Even my mother did not like me being so intense. My incessant discussions with her about the validity of the Bible only resulted in her displeasure with me. In my zeal, I also lost a number of friends who tired of my constant preaching to them. It wasn't long before I gave up spreading the word of the Bible because the price was too high. I decided that most people were just not ready to listen to the truth.

I eventually discovered that the Bible translation I listened to at Bible Camp differed slightly from the Catholic version. The passages that I found in the Catholic bible spoke very differently about the punishment of sinners. Uncovering this discrepancy raised all my unresolved issues with these teachings again.

I felt manipulated and lied to by this Christian organization and I wondered if the team leader had been lied to as well. I began to question his display of devotion to religion. Sadly, I realized that some of the Bible passages still did not make sense to me and my questions remained without answers.

Despite the perceived deception, I still knew in my heart that God existed and that He listened to us. I felt that the Bible was real but just not easily understood unless it had been studied in depth. I believed that Jesus was alive and I accepted Him as my Savior. I had deep faith that prayers worked and that there was life after death.

Years later, my spiritual explorations and life experiences expanded that initial perspective. I understood the whole idea of religion in a much wider universal context. My travels introduced me to Christians, Buddhists, Jews, Muslims, atheists and yogic gurus alike. I came to see them all as human beings observing life through their truth and I learned to be more tolerant and accepting of everyone as a result.

AWAKENING INSIGHT
God exists. He listens to us.
The Bible can be understood with advanced study.
Jesus is alive. There is life after death.
Prayer works...all you have to do is, ask
for a sign and be ready to listen.

These early moments prepared me to open to a truth about unseen realities that were far beyond my capability to know back then.

SECOND DOT

The Opportunity Created By Having A Good Education

Throughout my education, I understood that the first key to being successful in life and earning a good living was to attend reputable schools.

In primary school, I prepared well and obtained the good grades I needed to be accepted into one of the best high schools in Gdansk. Although my secondary school environment was very competitive, I was up to the challenge and completed high school in good standing.

At the age of nineteen, I took the next step into university. Once again I won out against the thousands of other applicants who were fighting for the few coveted openings at the more desirable and free public university. I was overjoyed at being accepted but I soon discovered the facility was very disappointing and its methodologies were quite poor.

At that time I was passionately focused on making music and I thought that a marketing degree would be useful to support my growing musical career. In the less than ideal environment, it did not take long before my interest in marketing was killed, which took the joy out of the experience for me. Despite this setback, I still earned a master's degree in Business Administration with a major in Marketing Management. The course material was relatively easy to understand which made it effortless to pass the exams. I even won a scholarship without having to work too hard.

This left me with plenty of time to devote to experimenting with and exploring my musical talents as well as affording me ample opportunity to meet many friends who helped shape my destiny. One in particular, Thomas, was responsible for my first trip to New York.

Looking back from my present position, I can see the power and influence that education holds in life. Without that experience, I would not have had the ability to earn a living while I was traveling. I would not have met the person who provided my first travel and work adventure to New York. And, I would not have had the credentials to teach at the university in Cali, Colombia where I now live.

AWAKENING INSIGHT
There are no accidents. Everything you experience in life has a meaningful purpose and has value.

THIRD DOT

The Importance Of Being True To Yourself And Following Your Passion

From my teenage years through post-university, I lived and breathed for music and performing onstage. There was no sacrifice that I wouldn't make in order to follow my obsession.

I sang, played guitar, composed music and was even recording with different rock bands at one point. My bands managed to win local music competitions and one of them signed a contract with Sony Music Poland. Needless to say this was a big deal for us and was the culmination of years of effort and dedication to our trade.

But, in a most disheartening turn of events, I had a serious disagreement with the manager of Sony Music Poland who was very well known in Polish show business circles. He also had his own band and I had the distinct impression he was jealous of our band's commercial success. The altercation started when I was unwilling to show enough appreciation for the Sony manager's band. Diplomacy was never my strong suit and as a result of my lack of acknowledgement to him, my band kicked me out before they signed the Sony contract.

The whole experience of having to leave the band, especially with such a high profile possibility in its near future made me angry as well as sad but I learned my lesson: no matter the consequences, I knew I had to always be true to myself and speak my words honestly.

Instead of getting depressed and being defeated by the experience, I quickly organized a new band, which did pretty well playing different gigs, and recording my songs. This band and I did quite well and had many good times that we shared. Ironically, my ex-band who signed with Sony had minimal success in selling their album, even though it had the heavy promotional clout of a big corporation behind it.

Performing in rock bands was a full-time passion that I lived 100%. My ability to work hard, my competitive nature, my inspiration to create and play music were the fuel that kept me focused on my goals and dreams. As difficult as it was to deal with the outcomes of my disagreement with the Sony manager, I knew that my honesty and integrity mattered more. These were and are the principles that guided me then and continue to do so today.

Fourth Dot

The Value In Taking Action, Working Hard And Being Present

As an amateur musician I had expenses. I wanted a new guitar, mini recording studio, and new microphones. I was looking for a summer job and asked my father if I could help him build houses in Germany. He agreed to hire me and I ended up working construction with him all summer holidays.

It was a challenging experience as my father was a strict boss and our accommodations were very basic - quite different from what I knew in Poland. For weeks, we labored through continuous fifteen -hour days including Sundays. I learned to work hard and not complain. Occasionally, we were able to take short breaks to visit the charming French villages that were close to the German border.

My father's work ethic and values caused him to be quite upset at people who were not employed.

He used to say, "The jobs are everywhere only some people don't want to work that hard. They just want easy solutions."

At the time, I agreed but later on, I came to understand that it wasn't that people didn't want to work hard or were just looking for the easy way out. It was more that they were filled with self-doubt and low self-esteem because they never had the opportunity to develop a more positive outlook. It was their inner negative dialog that kept them from stepping out and seeking employment. My father's own personal strength made it difficult for him to understand others who may not have been so well equipped for life's challenges.

Painting walls, replacing patchwork on the floor or scraping off old wallpaper was less than stimulating work. When I got bored, I would slow down and become unproductive. My father noticed this and would repeat the same phrase over and over again to me:

"When you are painting the wall only think about painting that wall. When you scrape the wallpaper, this should be the only thing you are focusing on."

I thought it was the most ridiculous saying at the time but years after, I understood the profound meaning in his words. Although my father was not a consciously spiritual person I considered him to be the best Zen teacher I ever knew. He unconsciously practiced such Zen principles in his life, which was probably one of the keys to his professional success and the respect that he gained in the village close to Kaiserslautern where he worked.

AWAKENING INSIGHT
You can practice Zen meditation at work by being focused and present on the task you are performing and only on that task.

Thanks to my father and the tough work I undertook in Germany, I was never afraid of not having a job. I intuitively knew that there would always be work for me whether it was an actual job or whether I created one. My time in Germany taught me a lot about stepping up, taking action, working hard and paying attention to the task at hand.

Many successful people say that attitude is important. I would say in the case of the job market and in life, attitude is *everything*.

AWAKENING INSIGHT
"Attitude is everything."

FIFTH DOT

Becoming Resilient And Following The Dream

During my fourth year at University, my first long-term girlfriend broke up with me and after a week of sadness and frustration I was ready to entertain new life opportunities.

Thomas, one of my schoolmates, had decided to spend his summer vacation in the U.S. and he invited me to join him. The goal was to do something different, have fun, practice English and make money so we could also travel across the States. Even though I did not know him very well, I wanted to put my relationship pain behind me so I jumped at the chance for an adventure. I bought my ticket the next day and organized an American visa a few weeks later.

Just before our departure, my girlfriend contacted me and wanted to reconcile. As I was still emotionally involved with her, I agreed to resume our relationship when I returned from my American adventure. I said goodbye and departed for the States.

I arrived in New York with a few dollars in my pocket, my tourist visa in hand and a place to stay at a friend's house. I quickly found two jobs, one in a bagel shop and the other at a construction company. Each workplace offered its unique, unexpected challenges. I severely injured my arm while working at a demolition site on the construction job and, at the bagel shop I was punched in the face by a Puerto Rican workmate who stole money from the register. Thankfully, everything was caught on camera and my experience gained me respect from the owner.

Despite the difficulties, I did not give up and kept working at both jobs to save enough money for the planned adventure that Thomas and I were eagerly awaiting to embark upon. I worked sixteen hours a day until I finally earned enough to finance my first road trip.

After much effort and perseverance, we were ready to enjoy the benefits of our summer's labor before returning to Poland. Thanks to the Drive-Away car rental company and its 'generous' provision of a well-used Toyota truck from its discount inventory, myself, Thomas, Thomas' pothead cousin and a female Polish student made our way from New York to Florida. The truck had the added decor of a palette of dead garden flowers in the back. We speculated and nervously joked about the possibility of pot being buried under the flowers and entertained ourselves with made up stories of the drugs belonging to the mafia. We imagined they would discover them and blame us for stealing the drugs. Then we made up stories of all the scary consequences of our mythical thievery. We created such a convincing tale we actually made ourselves so seriously afraid of what could be buried under the dead flowers that no one had the courage to even check it out.

In Florida, we hit all the tourist attractions – MGM Studios in Orlando, alligators and turtles in Everglades National Park, Daytona Beach and Miami. We were carefree and totally enjoying the moment of each new site. We made our way southern tip of Florida, Key West, where I was introduced to the relaxed vibe of the Caribbean coast. I completely fell in love with the slow pace and tropical weather of this area. I was fully ready to just go with the flow of life in this paradise but my friends chose to return to New York after only six days away. Sadly, I had no choice but to go with them.

That working summer in the U.S. was an educational experience and I returned to Poland confident and infused with a typical American 'can do' attitude of anything is possible.

AWAKENING INSIGHT
There is no limit to what is possible. If you work hard enough and stay focused on your goal - the sky's the limit.

My time in America also changed my obsession with becoming a musician. I read somewhere that Robert Plant from Led Zeppelin had decided to quit music if he hadn't achieved success by age 21. His philosophy made sense. As I was now 22 and the expected level of musical progress had not yet happened in my life, I decided to focus on my professional career.

In looking for work in my specific field, I chose to return to New York in hopes of finding an internship in marketing. My plan was to get back into marketing so I could add some practical expertise to my lacking resume and utilize my fresh Master's Degree in Business and Administration. With the experience I would gain in New York, I could then return to Poland and be a lucrative candidate for work with an international company.

A few days after obtaining my degree, I left Poland to return to New York. I had $400US in my pocket and the strong intention in my heart to follow through on my plan. I knew I could stay at my uncle's home in New York for free and it didn't take long to find a non-paying internship at a small marketing agency called The Innovation Works. Interning at The Innovation Works was a great experience. It allowed me to see the how business worked in America and it gave me a new perspective on what was possible in the field of marketing.

As I was about to learn, however, plans often take detours. My circumstances drastically changed when I was no longer able to stay with my uncle. He had emigrated from Poland to begin a new life in America and his living arrangements in New York did not easily accommodate me staying there for an extended amount of time. I was running out of money and with no more than $100 US, it was clear I had to let go of the idea of an internship and find paying work to survive.

Even though I had no experience as a waiter, I went from restaurant to restaurant with a fake resume asking for a job. I finally found my first employment at a Polish-American restaurant in the East End called, Cristina. I made my first dollars from tips there and found a shared room with two other guys at my workmate, Kasia's house. Because I still needed more money, I asked my new employer for extra hours. Apparently such forward behavior was frowned upon and I was fired on the spot. It was a mixed blessing as I was ready to go anyway.

There followed a series of short disastrous restaurant jobs that each ended in my either leaving or being let go. The reasons for my departures consisted of minor infractions of protocol, simple inexperience -not knowing how to open a wine bottle properly, my lack of having dessert items on the menu committed to memory and having the audacity to ask for full-time work. Neither the fact that I was prepared to work as hard as possible nor the undeniable truth that my customers seemed happy with me made any difference or seemed to matter. With each firing however, I did not give up or lose hope. I always believed that my dwindling finances would be replenished with a steady job somehow.

For some unknown reason, my ambition to become a well-paid waiter was not shared by those for whom I worked. I still remember my tall, skinny, fifty-something employer at a Moroccan restaurant and his response to my inquiry about a promotion to full-time work.

"You go. It is over! And don't you come back!" His empty grey eyes pierced through me as he spoke in broken English.

I reluctantly left that job without even getting my share of the massive tips that had been earned on my shift.

In all, I was sacked from four different restaurants. I did not know why it happened to me or what was wrong. Even though I had very little experience and my English was far from perfect, I had a really upbeat attitude and worked hard. In life so far, these qualities had been enough to propel me positively through other challenges but this time was different.

I remember making my way down 7th Avenue in Manhattan feeling downtrodden, desperate and very alone. The old gum and other debris that littered the smelly pavement seemed to reflect my state of mind. I felt as crushed and insignificant as the bits of garbage that dotted the sidewalk. As I walked with no intended direction, I began to pray to God for help, repeatedly saying the Lord's Prayer.

Before I knew it, I was standing outside one of the top Cantonese restaurants in Manhattan - Dish and Salt. It was located next door to the Fox TV Studios on 57th Street. I was familiar with this restaurant because my new roommate worked there as a bus boy. When I had visited him at the restaurant, I had instantly loved the atmosphere and connected easily with the managers who enjoyed my entertaining and funny songs.

Employment at this establishment seemed far above my skill level and I had been told that being Polish was a hindrance. But, in my present situation, I had nothing to lose so I applied anyway. I used my prior meeting of the managers to ask for an opportunity to work there and was overjoyed and shocked when they told me to come back the following day for training.

That lonely night in New York taught me two things: to believe in the power of the unseen hand of God in my life and to not let others decide for me what is possible and what is not.

AWAKENING INSIGHT
Believe in the power of the hand of God in your life.
Do not listen to others tell you what is possible and what is not.

On the first day of my training, the restaurant was filled to capacity as usual. The owner, a tense, impatient and well-dressed Chinese businesswoman from Hong Kong, nervously asked me to clear a recently deserted table and bring the dishes quickly to the kitchen. I had no schooling in the art of carrying big trays so I simply piled everything on the tray in no particular order, lifted it onto my shoulder and headed for the kitchen.

As I was making my way between the tables filled with customers, I felt some of the glasses that were full of wine shift position and fall to one side of the tray. I could not control the upset balance as the whole pile slid toward a well-dressed Chinese couple's table and the entire content landed on them. With the crashing sound of broken glass, the entire restaurant went silent. All eyes were on me. My colleagues erupted into laughter as the owner immediately swung into action. She apologized to the couple and offered them compensation for their trouble.

Despite my deafening inner criticism and my fear that I had lost yet another restaurant job, nothing happened. I came back the next day and happily worked there until the last days of my visa. I even managed to save a few thousand dollars from the tips I received.

Some of our clients included corporate executives from Fox Television whose offices were next door. One such regular was Rupert Murdoch. Sometimes he would arrive with a cast of characters that looked like they were straight out of the Good Fellas movie. They would sit together drinking double espressos, smoking cigars and talking business.

I loved to serve them and after learning, with the help of their sarcasm, how to serve a proper espresso, I warmed up to them and felt comfortable enough to strike up a spontaneous conversation one day.

"You guys remind me of my favorite actors from Good Fellas, Joe Pesci and the other guy." I offered.

"Joe is actually one of my best friends and my favorite actor as well." This came from one of the Armani-suited men who puffed intently on his oversized Cuban cigar. He looked like he could have been Pesci's twin.

"I love the way they speak. Do you mind if I improvise?"

They looked at me with surprised interest as I bantered on without waiting for an answer. I rolled into a dialogue with them in my best 'Good Fellas' Italian Mafia dialect that was strangely mixed with my Polish accent:

"Whot de fock is goin' on here? I don' give a shit whot you talkin' about! Drink your damn espresso 'cause I'm not gonna waste my time waiting for ..." and then I suddenly realized that I had taken the improv a bit over the edge.

The Pesci 'twin' looked in my eyes with an expressionless face. I couldn't tell if he was about to hire me or kill me. His mate however was red-faced and had tears of laughter rolling down his cheeks.

"I am sorry I went too far, nothing personal." I quickly left the table embarrassed by my behavior yet somehow proud at my bravado.

AWAKENING INSIGHT
Be bold and push the boundaries of
social acceptance. It can take you far and create
unexpected opportunities which open doors.

My performance earned me a triple tip and from that moment on, I became their main waiter. I am sure that if I had stayed longer in New York, I would have ended up with a career at Fox Television or somewhere in the entertainment business but my plan and my life were focused in a different direction.

I enjoyed my new job but being a waiter while having a Master's Degree in Business was not the best option long term. During my time in New York City I was constantly looking for inspiration and thinking about what I really wanted to do with my life.

During lunch breaks I would scan the Help Wanted column in local papers and from that, I realized most of the jobs and professional courses were related to either graphic design, multimedia or programming. It was right after the Dot Com crash in 2000 and many of my restaurant colleagues who had lost money investing in the stock market were waiting tables and taking IT courses on their days off. I asked God for guidance.

Soon after, my uncle invited me to dinner where I was introduced to his best friend, Janus. Janus was a professional magician who had turned his passion into a world-famous successful career. While he was amusing me with his mind-blowing magic tricks that evening, I asked him what were his most important life lessons. His eyes flashed with confident wisdom as he answered that being open, following your own path and doing what you loved were principles that had been his lifelong guidance.

AWAKENING INSIGHT
"Be open to new life possibilities.
Do not expect your friends to follow you in your
life choices. Always do what you love."
~ Janus

This was exactly what I needed to hear. Once again, my prayers were answered.

I began to visit my uncle more often as I was missing my family in Poland a great deal. I shared with him my findings about the IT job market and asked him if he knew anyone who might be able to help me explore further. He indicated that one of his neighbors worked in IT but he didn't particularly like this man and they did not speak to each other. On my next visit to see my uncle, a synchronous moment intervened to boost my progress.

I happened to arrive at the exact moment the IT neighbor had chosen to be out working in his garden. It is a rare occurrence for people in New York to interact with each other but this was one of those rare moments. On the spur of the moment, my uncle went over to him and asked him if he would chat with me about his profession. Steve was extremely helpful and our chat stretched into hours of conversation about my passions, my dreams and what IT position might best suit me.

"I think web design would be the most suitable position for you. You have an artistic soul as well as ample analytical skills." He said after our long sharing.

I thanked him and knew it was another sign from God. I began to pursue studies to become a web designer. I bought some discounted books about web design and a cheap laptop from my friend. The last months of my American Dream was spent studying the basics of HTML and graphic design.

When I consider this whole New York experience, I can see how each event was a pointer on the map that guided me to my next destination. The synchronicities flowed abundantly everywhere.

From losing my free accommodations with my uncle, to the series of restaurant jobs that eventually led me to the prosperous experience at the Cantonese establishment, to the chance meeting with my uncle's disliked IT neighbor whose conversation ultimately provided me with the means to sustain myself on my world travels – the nudge of the invisible guidance that I sought was always moving me to the next level of development.

Each setback and challenge taught me how to be resilient and self-reliant and how to use my inner resources and talents to thrive.

AWAKENING INSIGHT

If you don't know what to do with your life ask God for guidance. If you don't believe in God, ask the Universe. If you don't believe in anything, ask your own inner wisdom for an answer before you go to sleep.
Trust there will be a response. Notice your experiences. Observe how the answers appear.

Sixth Dot

A New Passion –Tenacity & Fortitude –Building Skills And Knowledge

When I returned to Poland, I bought the latest model computer and spent every single hour studying web design from the books I had purchased in New York. I was so intensely focused on my new career that I rarely even left the house. I continually searched for official higher education in the field of Graphic or Web Design but the only course I found was about programming in C++ and Unix administration. At that time in Poland, it was virtually impossible to obtain any certified education in web design because the Dot Com crash of 2000 resulted in no interest or trust in anything to do with the Internet. So, I kept my pursuits a secret and shared them with no one. No matter what others were saying, I had learned to listen to my inner wisdom and I was sure there was a bright future in my choice.

Internet access was expensive and the service was extremely slow so I studied with anyone who was willing to share his knowledge with me for free. I was lucky to have many friends who knew a lot about designing websites. I managed to ask questions and learn from them while still keeping my ultimate plans to myself. They became my first teachers.

AWAKENING INSIGHT
*In order to achieve worldly goals it is important in the early
stages to be very persistent. Trust your own inner knowing.
Do not share your dreams with others to
avoid criticism and negative energy.*

After a few months of continual study, I was able to set up the first website for my portfolio.

One of my dearest and oldest friends, Michal Lange*, was particularly supportive. He was a professional graphic designer who worked for one of the famous IT companies in Poland. He clearly recognized my passion and after a few lessons with him, he recommended me for a position as a junior web designer at one of the agencies. It was the first professional experience of my new career and I was thrilled to have the opportunity. Sadly, the company was in financial difficulties and had to let a number of employees go. I was among the group who was fired.

* *Michal Lange died in the car crash accident when I was in Colombia. We grew up in the same neighborhood and he influenced my pop-culture taste and sense of humor. He was there to help me find my first job after coming back from U.S.; he arranged for me to stay at his friend's house in London when I moved there. I am eternally grateful for his help and friendship and I hope that one day our souls will have a chance to meet each other again.*

AWAKENING INSIGHT
*Be passionate, some people will acknowledge it and
help you to make your dreams come true.*

Instead of giving up, I updated my portfolio and resume and sent it out to all the Help Wanted ads I could find. It wasn't long before I had a new opportunity available to me.

My new boss was impressed with my work but insisted that I also become the administrator for the in-house Unix System. I knew little about Unix but found someone to explain the basics to me and with a few private classes, I felt ready and comfortable to add that responsibility to my job description.

AWAKENING INSIGHT
Even if you don't have enough knowledge or experience,
take advantage of all the possibilities that life offers you.
Learn to say, "yes" to everything.

I kept learning about web design on my own and never stopped taking advantage of every opportunity to advance my new skills and use the ones I had already absorbed. In order to improve my graphic design expertise, I took various freelance jobs on the side to build my portfolio. Even my programming and IT studies from university turned out to be useful as that knowledge provided the depth and diversity to help me keep my job.

After a year, it was time to expand my horizons. I started to look for new job opportunities. The opportunity soon appeared. I was hired by an internet/multimedia agency, Begroup. The pay was better and the projects were far more interesting. In short order, I was promoted to senior web designer and became an art director as well. My resume was improving and my portfolio started to look professional. The goal I started to focus on before I left for the U.S. was beginning to bear fruit and I was thoroughly satisfied with the evolution of my work life. Looking back on the process, I realized how every challenge every victory and every step had brought me to this point of personal achievement and success. To me, my joy and sense of fun at work was a clear sign that my choices were made in alignment with my purpose.

It took a lot of dedication to my goals to achieve what I did but I was well-equipped for the experience. I learned to develop a great deal of fortitude through the process of my self-education. It was a quality that saved me many times during my world travels.

AWAKENING INSIGHT
Keep on educating yourself.
Put forth every effort to pursue your passion.
Trust that your inspiration to make changes in
your life is guidance from your soul.

SEVENTH DOT

Love Is The Most Powerful Force In The Universe

Although I was having a lot of fun at work, my long-term relationship was suffering. When I was in the U.S., I knew my girlfriend was waiting for me and I missed her a great deal. What I felt for her was deep and real enough that I was prepared to let go of potential possibilities and return to Poland for the sake of our relationship. We had been happily reunited when I returned so it came as quite a shock when she broke up with me a second time.

She informed me that she was leaving me for another man. It was hard to let her go, as I trusted her completely and felt very close to her. At the same time, a part of me was relieved. I was not ready for marriage and she had been putting pressure on me for a long time.

AWAKENING INSIGHT
Don't get married if you are not 100 percent inspired to do so. It might take time but trust that you will find the love that you have always dreamed about.

I worked full-time during the day but after the end of my relationship, my evenings were reserved for partying and meeting women. Sex and alcohol dulled my loneliness and calmed my frustration. Even a temporary version of relationship momentarily comforted the emptiness. However, this unhealthy lifestyle had consequences as I eventually became ill with asthma. At night, my incessant coughing was so intense, I was sure I would never recover.

When I met a crazy dreamer named Monica, the symptoms disappeared. My life changed and felt less frenzied which helped my healing on many levels. In addition to changing my party-going habits, love or its absence was a powerful driving force in my life that had already influenced my travel to New York and my return to Poland. It was soon to exert its influence again.

Monica and I quickly fell in love and even though she lived a great distance (an eleven hour train ride from Sopot where I lived), we made it work. Even though we missed each other a great deal, we would send passionate text messages, chat on the Internet and eagerly wait for our next meeting. These moments became the focus of my life and my favorite activities.

AWAKENING INSIGHT
Follow your heart.
It has a wisdom that will lead you to your most
profound destiny. In the long term it pays off.

When she was about to graduate from University, Monica informed me with a tone of impatience,

"I want to go to another country. There are no jobs here. I am thinking of going to the U.S."

"Well, it sounds good to me but I am not sure I want to go back to the US." I remarked.

The memories of working at the restaurants, the bagel shop and demolition site flooded my thoughts. Even though I left as a professional web designer, I had no desire to repeat any aspect of that painful and exhausting learning curve.

"Let me update my portfolio and I will send emails to explore where there might be jobs available." I offered.

It was February 2004, just three month before Poland joined the European Union, which would allow Polish citizens to work in the UK without a visa. I quickly updated my portfolio and wrote an email template introducing myself and sharing my credentials.

I visited hundreds of web design agency sites from all over the world and sent a slightly personalized version of my email to each of the companies. I felt so inspired and laser focused on the mission that I breezed through the work in about two hours.

The very next day I received a few replies - one from Hong Kong, one from Belgium, one from Canada and five from England, mostly from London. What surprised me the most was receiving so many positive replies from England. The UK would never have been my first choice for relocation. I was not a fan of their mostly dreary weather and I had not felt very welcome when I tried to visit my friends for a few days on my return from New York. Immigration officials had asked many annoying questions of me, had ultimately refused me entry and had stamped my passport as such. It caused me numerous problems later in my travels. Add to that my perception of the stereotypical British personality that was stoical and rather aloof and the UK did not get my impassioned vote as my next place to live.

I told Monica about the emails and possible directions. I signed up for Skype and started conversations with my potential employees. After a few weeks of dialogue with various companies, I decided to set aside my mental biases against the UK and give it a try. I organized five different interviews in London. My plan was to visit one company each day and convince each that I was the right person for the job. There was no question in my mind that I would be hired by one of them.

Without having any guarantee of a job, I told my current Polish employer that I was leaving. He was supportive of my exploration and wished me good luck. I bought a bus ticket from Gdansk to London. The trip one-way would take a grueling twenty-four hours to destination but I was so intent on my mission that I barely gave it a thought.

The next week I said good-bye to my boss, my parents and Monica. She was to join me few months later after she finished her final semester at university.

Dressed in the only suit I owned, I boarded the bus and found a seat among the many working class fellow-dreamers: waitresses, builders, plumbers, bartenders and au pairs. Although everyone had the same goal of making their fortune in the UK, my professional experience as a web designer and the fact that I had actual job interviews lined up made me feel like I was in another league compared to the other passengers. I felt like I could conquer the world.

After the long and tiring trip, we reached the immigration border in Dover. The trouble began almost immediately. I was asked a few questions and was then told to go to another room and wait for an interview with an immigration officer. I settled into a seat in the crowded room that was filled with an eclectic mixture of people from as far away as Africa and Asia and waited for my interview. It was two hours before I was finally called and I assumed my bus had probably left for London without me. I felt that something was wrong.

"Mr. Ziolkowski, what are you going to do in London? We found resumes in your backpack. Do you know you are not allowed to work legally in UK?" They asked me with the polite but soulless British manner I remembered from my earlier encounter years ago.

"I am only going for interviews. Employers want to meet me personally. Here is the letter from one of the companies." I showed them the letter I had received.

Knowing that I had a stamp in my passport that signified my denial of entry before, I had asked one of the potential employers to send me an invitation letter just in a case I needed it. I silently thanked my father for teaching me to be ready for all possible situations in life.

"But the letter shows the wrong date, Mr. Ziolkowski. We are in February and the letter points into July. How can you explain that?" They asked as they passed the letter back to me.

"Let me see...indeed it is a mistake." I stared at the letter in disbelief and could not figure out how I had not noticed this before now.

Clearly I was trapped and had no idea what to do. The officers attempted to contact the business but it was Saturday and no one was at the office on a weekend. They sent me back to the waiting room and hours later I was called back by them again to receive their decision:

"Mr. Ziolkowski, you are denied entry to the UK." They declared.

"What?!" I was shocked and panicked. All I could think about were the lost interviews, returning home feeling like a loser, and having to start everything from scratch again. It was beyond depressing.

"You can go to the UK Embassy in Poland and provide sufficient documentation to change your status. Good luck!" the officer offered while crossing out the entry stamp in my passport. With the stroke of a pen, my entire future vaporized before my eyes.

I felt completely drained. The exhausting bus ride, the hours of waiting and this repeat rejection ordeal suddenly caught up with me as I left the immigration office still on the French side of the border. I was advised to wait outside for the bus to take me back home to Poland. It was about minus five degrees. I felt the cold penetrate my body as I waited more hours in the shivering cold. My throat started to hurt and I was completely numb. The bus finally arrived from London headed for Gdansk and I started the return trip home.

I was not the same confident, self-assured passenger who had first boarded this bus on the way to the UK. As I collapsed into the nearest empty seat, the crisp luster of my suit and my equally positive outlook were showing the effects of the unpleasant experiences of the day. My head down, my heart heavy, I thought about the implications of what had just happened. I had been eager to move to London and find work for Monica's sake.

My love for her and my desire to look after our relationship had driven me beyond my comfort zone and into the devastating rejection I had just suffered. Opportunities were shattered and the dream of Monica and I living together in mutual joy and prosperity were universes away at this moment. I fell into an exhausted sleep.

~

As I look back on that pivotal moment of rejection now, I recognize a familiar pattern of taking action because of my emotional connections with the women in my life. It had been at the heart of my trip to New York with Thomas when my first relationship had ended. It had also drawn me back to Poland to be with her again.

But beyond the desire for a meaningful, healthy relationship, there was a deeper thread that defined this pattern. I could not identify it back then but I felt it very strongly and it could not be ignored. It was a fiery longing for the most powerful unifying force in the Universe – LOVE.

I know now that my travels were inspired partially by a search for that deep and lasting love in my life. Back then however, I could not have known the way in which I would discover that kind of love. This latest UK disaster and its motivating energy were yet another example of learning about true love in my usual way – by challenge, trial and exploration.

Ahead there were other adventures more intense than my UK rejection but without the power from that deeper need for connection that burned in me even then, I doubt my steps would have taken me so many miles from my homeland and taught me so much.

EIGHTH DOT

When One Door Closes Another One Opens

When I awoke from my restless sleep and collected my thoughts, I sent text messages to my family and my girlfriend telling them what had happened. After another 24-hour journey, I arrived back home and showed the incriminating letter to my mom as I explained the reason for my rejection from the UK. As I was looking again at the letter, it struck me that I needed to let the company know what had happened as well. I scanned the letter, which included an explanation of why I would be meeting with them and emailed it to the owner in London. I also cancelled the other interviews I had scheduled and sent a similar explanatory message.

Al and Nick from Prismix, the company whose mistake had started the avalanche of problems in my plans, replied immediately to my message:

> Fil, we are so sorry for what happened. We made a terrible mistake with the date and apologize for any problems this caused you. On a good note, we have decided we would like to work with you online. Can you send us your rates?

I replied with my per diem rate of 100 GBR for the standard 8-hour Polish workday. The British currency was very strong at that time, so making 100 quid a day was a great opportunity especially taking into account the low cost of living in Poland. They agreed to my terms and sent me a contract.

As I had already moved out of my apartment in Sopot before leaving for the UK, I decided to continue my adventure and asked Monica to find me accommodation in Cracow where she was studying. I spent two days with my family and took the train to Cracow. I remember awkwardly lugging my big PC case and a massive old type monitor along with all my baggage as I boarded the train. It must have been quite a sight for my fellow passengers to observe.

The next day, I started working online for Prismix in London and one other company in Canada. I also had received positive responses from the other London companies who indicated that they would wait for me while I dealt with my visa situation. I could never have known these amazing results were waiting for me out of the disastrous events that preceded them.

AWAKENING INSIGHT

Always look for the bright side of life. When the one door closes another is in the process of opening.

I worked as a freelancer knowing that within three short months, Poland was going to join the European Union. Then, I would be able to work in London legally without any immigration issues. All I had to do was be patient, and wait for the right time to try again.

The time flew by. In the meantime, I was spending quality moments with my girlfriend, making good money online, improving my portfolio, exploring the captivating beauty of Cracow and soaking in its famous artistic vibe. Given the positive outcomes that emerged out of my dark experience with the UK immigration, I would happily accept the incorrectly dated letter again if it meant creating this same result. Everything had happened for a reason and in universal perfection.

Ninth Dot

The Value Of Second Chances - Returning To The UK

AWAKENING INSIGHT
Preparation is the key.

Three months later, the owners from Prismix bought me a one-way plane ticket to London. Prior to my departure, I visited the immigration office in Poland and declared my passport lost in order to receive a new one without the troublesome stamp in it. I was taking no chances and had learned my lesson from past experiences.

This second chance to work in the UK held the promise and feel of success. The vast step up in the mode of transportation certainly reflected possibility. Because I had taken the time to prepare and was more sure-footed in my abilities, I was optimistic that everything would unfold without any trouble.

At Heathrow airport, I was curious to see if my immigration situation had changed since the last refusal. I assumed my information was stored in their computer so I took a chance and bravely showed them the old passport with the rejection notification in it.

"Welcome to the UK, Mr. Ziolkowski." I heard from the officer.

"Thank you, sir. Does this mean that I am legally in the UK and do not need to worry about being turned back?" I held my breath.

"Mr. Ziolkowski, we have just updated our data system with your current information. You are allowed to work in the UK." the officer smiled at me as he handed me back my passport. It was music to my ears. I felt all the tension drain from my body and a giddy sense of victory flood through me.

I arrived in London with a couple of British pounds in my pocket hoping to pick up where I had left off in my quest for the best employment possible. I had a few interviews set up with the businesses I had contacted earlier and was optimistic about making my fortune soon.

Thanks to my friend Michal, who had helped me in the beginning of my web design career, I was able to stay temporarily at his ex-lover's apartment. The rent was cheap and Gosia, Michal's ex-girlfriend, was a very sweet and helpful woman. In addition to taking good care of me by feeding me well, she took time to show me around London and introduced me to the magic of the city. Because of Gosia's generosity, I had a little money in my pocket and a few snacks in my backpack and was able to visit all the companies I had found where I might seek employment.

AWAKENING INSIGHT
Never underestimate the power of good relationships.
Maintain and nurture your friendships because they are part
of your interdependent learning and support system in life.

Finding my first job in London was not as easy as I assumed it would be. My English was still quite limited and after all the interviews with the companies who had expressed interest when I was in Poland, I had been told in a rather polite manner that they would 'get back to me'. I waited days with no response from them.

The key consultation was with a woman named, Anney, who was from a recruitment agency. Even if I did not know how to pronounce 'Leicester Square' which was the location of her office, she was impressed with all the references and documents I provided. Anney promised to call me when an opening was available.

The lack of employment, took its toll on my money supply which was almost all spent. Monica and I were planning to live together in London and she was expected to arrive from Poland soon. I barely had adequate funds for food let alone the finances to rent a room or help her find a job.

I prayed to God for guidance. The answer rose up almost immediately from that familiar intuitive voice within me. I could contact Prismix again and offer to give them a free sample of my work on one of their projects. They knew my work online but had no experience of me in real time. That way, I could demonstrate the quality of my skills and let them know I was available for employment. I wasted no time making my way to their location that day and asked them to give me a design task to complete which I offered to do for free. Two hours later with the assignment completed, and after a short chat, I left the premises with a temporary job.

Initially I was paid weekly and earned enough to rent a room including the up-front deposit. I moved to the Elephant and Castle district of London, which was a rather dirty and hectic neighborhood close to the center of London.

I shopped often at Tesco, which was a massive multinational grocery and merchandise store near my new living quarters. In order to get there, I needed to walk into a dark tunnel that felt very scary to pass through and cross a very noisy and busy street. The route also took me past a Colombian Cultural Center. The Center included an attached restaurant whose windows were decorated with colorful flyers advertising Salsa dance lessons. It was a wisp of my future making its way to me through the universe.

Colombia never received good press in Europe due to its history of cocaine cartels and violent guerilla wars. Every time I passed by the Center, I noticed fear rising in me as a result of all I had been told and believed about the culture and the country.

The subtle hand of universal irony was at work in my life. Despite my conditioned reactions and fears about Colombia, I actually chose to stop traveling and live there. It points out the value of firsthand experience rather than reacting to hearsay.

While Colombia would not be considered a safe country to live, I have found it not to be as dangerous as I believed when I lived in London and was influenced by all the negative press. Today, life goes on here like anywhere else in the world and like living or traveling, a healthy dose of common sense is key to maintaining your personal safety.

AWAKENING INSIGHT

Most fears are only a mental fantasy created by our mind, media or society. In order to move beyond the irrational fear, experience firsthand and decide for yourself what is worth your angst.

As I settled into my life in London, I learned to open to the power of prayer and to listen to my intuition. It had become an inner ally upon which I relied. Despite my fear, I proactively took the necessary steps to find work and push myself beyond my perceived limitations. My actions resulted in a whole new professional and social life. It was well worth the supreme effort it took.

Tenth Dot

Loneliness And The Corporate Life

Monica finally arrived in London and for the first time since we met, we were sharing the same space on a daily basis. Being in small quarters and in a foreign country was a great test for our relationship. It gave us an opportunity to see how much we understood each other and if we could maintain our romantic connection under the less than ideal circumstances.

She had difficulty finding work due to her limited English and high job expectations. At one point, we discussed the idea that she could become a model. I created a simple website for her, with photos that caused more problems than they solved. The only job offers she received from the website were from horny Londoners who had nothing to offer other than sexual propositions.

She complained about the weather and the people and everything that was wrong with London. I, however, was discovering how much I had grown to like London but I was not able to admit that in front of her. Before long, she started hating the city. I found myself becoming stressed about our deteriorating situation, which included my jealousy of the unwanted advances made toward her by other men. She began receiving phone calls from men she had barely met and I did not know what to do about it.

Instead of enjoying our place and the fact that we were together, I started feeling frustrated with our circumstances. As much as I wanted to improve our living situation, I didn't make enough money to move us to a nicer area and a bigger apartment.

When Monica finally did find a job, it was at a nightclub, which just made things even worse. I was working in the daytime Monday to Friday while she was working at night from Tuesday to Sunday. We hardly saw each other and our paths started to go in different directions. The intense romantic love we had shared was gone forever and because of that, I was slowly losing my self-confidence and my natural exuberance about life.

AWAKENING INSIGHT
Jealousy in a relationship is usually a sign of a problems and a symptom of a lack of self-esteem.

At the end of September 2004, my friend Niklas, CEO of Prismix, announced to me that they did not have enough clients to cover the costs of my employment so they had to let me go. The timing could not have been worse as my income stream was in serious danger without the paycheck from Prismix.

The company was struggling to survive and a few months after I left, it disappeared from the market.

In a crazy cosmic opening and closing of the doors of opportunity, just a few hours after I was let go from Prismix, I received a call from Anney at the recruitment agency where I had had my first interview in London. She asked if I was working and would I be interested in a well-paying position as a web designer/developer at a large IT firm. I did not let on that I was jobless as of a few hours before. I agreed to an interview that was set up for the following day. It was the first phone call I received about a job interview since Prismix... Right on time...spot on.

AWAKENING INSIGHT
*Magic works. Some call it synchronicity.
I believe that angels surround and take care of us.*

The interview went well and I was hired. After a few months, I was thoroughly enjoying my new career and feeling more relaxed. However, the tension in my relationship had reached the breaking point. Monica and I parted company in a very unpleasant way. Our romance was over and without her being in my life nothing was worthwhile. I lost my loving partner and with her departure, all the plans we had made to buy a house in Sopot by the beach were gone as well.

I became deeply depressed. The only thing that kept me going was my job and that became less inspiring too. Even though my work had landed me in an ideal situation and I was now making good money, the reason for doing so was no longer a part of my life. I did not know what to do and felt completely powerless to change anything that had happened.

After months of despair, my old reactive party habits surfaced. I began going out every night and looking up potential new women on dating sites. I decided it was time to learn better English so I set out to find a new English girlfriend and improve my language. I went on many dates and collected plenty of phone numbers but I was both numb and hurting from the loss of Monica and was unable to love anyone including myself.

I subconsciously compared each girl to her and no one measured up. I missed our intimate connection, the comfort of being in love with her and building our life together. Being with any other woman only made me feel unhappier and more alone and lonely.

Every date left me with a greater sense of emptiness and sadness. I had my share of international women to go out with - the Colombian woman who was offended and walked out on me at a restaurant because I asked about the cocaine issues in her native country; the Russian girl who showed way too much interest in luxurious lifestyle of London bankers. I tried to date French, Irish, English, Czech, Romanian, Japanese, Spanish, Brazilian and even Somalia women. I was looking for someone to fix my brokenness but none of them had the magic to erase the heartbreak I was carrying.

It wasn't just my personal relationship issues that were responsible for the dating scene as it was. It was also a cultural norm of the trendy, corporate scene in London as well. The culture was all about the chase for money, new restaurants, drugs, expensive toys, celebrity status, designer clothes and trivial gossip. In that environment, the potential to develop an authentic relationship seemed non-existent. The pace was too hectic. There was too little time and too many options. Being cool and living the city life in London became synonymous with frenzy, fakeness and loneliness.

AWAKENING INSIGHT
Relationships based on needing someone to make you happy never work. Happiness and love cannot be found outside oneself.

I spiraled down into continuous unhappiness with no relief from the gloom. Even my work about which I had initially been so passionate had become boring. The routine was killing me.

Every day it was the same monotony:

Wake up; take the same bus; stare at the same grumpy people staring at their mobile phones; line up at Starbucks for morning coffee; say, "All right" to everyone's empty inquiry about my wellbeing as we crowded together in the lift; finally get to my desk, turn on my computer and check emails; go to meetings, do some web design work and then time for lunch. At lunch, chat about business or make small talk. After lunch, come back to the office, send some more emails and do some work, then leave for the day. Go to a pub; get offered a round of beer; have a chat with your mates; get drunk; meet more random people and exchange phone numbers knowing you will never call them back; come back home alone and go to bed;

wake up the next morning and start the whole routine all over again ... that was my corporate life.

AWAKENING INSIGHT
"Too many people spend money they haven't earned, to buy things they don't want, to impress people they don't like."
~ Will Rogers

I tried desperately to get on with things. For sake of change I decided to move to another apartment in one of the coolest neighborhoods in London called, Angel. It was closer to work and, as I shared the apartment with two Australian women I could practice my English. Unfortunately, the cultural differences between us were so vast that I quickly let go of any notion of improving my English with them. We had little in common and they did not even get along with each other very well. Their constant bickering created a less than emotionally warm and open environment. Our conversations were minimal and I was not encouraged to participate further than simple talk with them.

Making new friends never really happened in London the same way it did in Poland. It was rare to make deep connections and, although I pretended that everything was fine, deep in my heart I was feeling disengaged and longing for an authentic conversation about something that mattered to me. I was not doing well at all.

After two years at my job that earned me both superstar level recognition and hefty pay raises, I started to feel burned out.

Every day it seemed I was asking myself, "What is the point of this life?"

I had it easy and lived like a king in one of the most inspiring cities in the world. I had no shortage of entertainment available to me. I ate exotic foods at international restaurants, went to concerts with my favorite bands, had access to theater and world class sporting events. I had the opportunity to get to know influential business managers from some of the top media brands in the world. But, at the end of the day I felt empty and anxious. The only way I could go to sleep was by consuming beer so I could calm down. I could not remember when I last went to sleep without having alcohol in my blood.

Although my life in London provided me with many gifts, there was a profound lesson being shown to me. The chain of events that had unfolded to bring me to this point were responsible for showing me that something was missing and that 'something' was what I needed to discover.

ELEVENTH DOT

Discovering Spirituality

My life felt the lack of love in it. I was discouraged and frustrated at my seeming inability to find the kind of relationship I wanted and needed to bring me happiness again. I kept in touch with my former Polish flat mates and other Polish friends who had moved to London also. The time I shared with them was comforting to me even though our conversations did not resolve or cure my emptiness or my broken heart.

In an attempt to heal my aching soul, I decided to download to my I-Pod every motivational talk and meditation I could find. I listened to them during lunch breaks at work. It got to the point where I couldn't wait for noon to come so I could go to the park near my office, sit in the beauty of the outdoors and absorb the next meditation or spiritual inspiration.

This was the beginning of my self-directed spiritual therapy. I remember reading an audiobook by an author with a strange Indian sounding name, Deepak Chopra. I was fascinated by his talks about the Seven Spiritual Law of Success. Although I was a believer in Christianity, I found his words very inspiring and not in conflict with my religious beliefs.

At that time I had no idea who Deepak Chopra was but his lectures made me feel relaxed and somehow comforted. I also had discovered and downloaded deep relaxation meditations that helped calm me down whenever I would start thinking of Monica.

I am very grateful to the virtual teachers who decided to publish their work on the Internet and thank the virtual pirates who shared their files on KaZaA. These people saved my life and led me to discoveries I would never have made without them.

A few months later, I was exploring on Google Video and happened to find a spiritual work called, "The Secret". For the first time in my life I heard someone talk seriously about creating reality with thought. I found this very attractive and inspiring. The concept of 'ask and it will be given' sounded wonderful and I felt like something new was being revealed right in front of me. Of course I wanted to try it out and at a certain point I had my chance and was overjoyed at the results.

It seemed like the route to my conscious new life view was brought about by 'international conspiracy'. I couldn't help but notice that I was able to get in touch with Eastern philosophy thanks to three American companies, Microsoft (operating system), Apple (I-Pod) and Google (streaming video) and peer-to-peer technology designed by Estonian programmers.

Step by step, my new spiritual education motivated me to expand my horizons and try new experiences that I would otherwise never have considered. For instance, I decided to go to my first Yoga class at a local sports center. One of my first teachers was a hippy looking character with tattoos and dreadlocks. Despite his outward appearance, he turned out to be one of the best Yoga teachers I ever met. I loved his powerful classes, which helped me feel happier and more connected to myself and to my soul.

Beyond the yoga interest, I also discovered that we had a lot in common. He was from Scotland and we both shared a passion for football. He was a big fan of the Celtic Glasgow team, whose two key players were Polish. He totally changed my perception of gurus as I had always pictured them to be old bearded men who talked nonsense and charged way too much money for their gimmicky talks. Instead, here was someone who loved football and who could not have looked less like a spiritual guide and yet he provided profoundly moving yoga classes. This was my introduction to Eastern philosophy.

Soon after, I met Kinga. She was a Polish girl who worked at Subway in less than ideal conditions yet she was always smiling and in good spirits. She was cute and smart, and spoke good English and was one of the happiest people I have ever met. As I got to know her, I discovered the secret to her wellbeing was because she was a practicing Buddhist and meditation was a regular part of her day. She called these the best activities on earth. Of course, I wanted to know more.

I asked her out and she invited me to the Diamond Way Buddhist Center with her. I found its approach to spirituality to be too westernized and not to my liking. The energy of the people there and the community in general seemed driven to party and indulge the same way that I had already experienced with Londoners. It was not my path but it started my first steps into exploring the other side of spirituality and opened me to be more aware of the new possibilities that were out there to be investigated.

I began to notice a shift in my inner energy and externally, I started to attract many new and interesting people into my life. As I had not found peace in the teachings of the Bible or in church, I started to question the radical Christian dogma I had been fed since I was a child. The everyday problems that people experienced never seemed to be solved by the religious approach which felt totally out of touch with modern life. Without question, my awareness was beginning to change and it was a welcome fresh start.

My depression was lifting slowly and one day, I went to Borders bookstore in search of other publications by this Deepak Chopra man I had discovered. I was shocked to find an entire bookshelf filled with his teachings. While I had thoroughly enjoyed his audio talks, I could not understand a single word in any of his books. The concepts did not make sense to me and the language was too sophisticated. A bit disappointed, I wandered over to the travel section.

As I was scanning travel books and enjoying the world they were exposing, something triggered in my mind and I remembered that *I had always wanted to travel*. It had been my biggest dream when I was younger. I recalled how much that desire had inspired me. I thought about the map I had put up on my wall and the places I had pinned. I had totally forgotten that I wanted to travel the world!

With all the money I saved during my last two years of working in London, it was now possible to do. It seemed that the 'somehow' I wondered about long ago had been resolved. But there was one problem that remained. Traveling the world still seemed like mission impossible that was only available to the chosen ones.

TWELFTH DOT

Pursuing My Dream

I always thought that becoming a world traveler was reserved for a special talented few globetrotters. It was a lifestyle only for those who had the courage to risk diving into the unknown and exposing themselves to the danger of this activity.

At one of the social evenings after work, I happened to have a conversation with a work mate, who I took to be quite an average guy. I was surprised and intrigued to hear that, prior to being hired by the company, he had taken an entire year off to travel the world.

"Perhaps there is less exclusivity to this travel process than I thought." I mused.

I investigated further and discovered that the practice of taking such a world tour was quite common in the UK. It even had a name and many young people used to take this so-called 'Gap Year' after graduating from university and before starting their careers. It was hardly the elitist pastime I thought it was. I could feel the excitement within me mounting with this new revelation.

I went to Borders bookstore to research further and found two books: "My First Time Around The World" by Lonely Planet and "Around The World" by Rough Guide. After reading them and a few other books on the subject, I was convinced I could give it a try.

However, I came from a country where it was customary to always travel with someone and none of my friends were in a position to join me. They were either busy, broke, not risk takers or just involved in other projects. Practically speaking, I had two choices. I either had to go on my own or not go at all.

Not long after that realization, I spoke to two workmates Steve, an Australian, and Gladys, an English citizen, about my passion. I confessed my concerns about traveling alone. They convinced me that I should go on my own as they usually did. From what I knew of them, they were not exceptional in terms of being adventurous or crazy so I was convinced that if they could do it, so could I.

Encouraged by the conversation I immediately got started. Through Skyscanner and Hostelbookers I booked flights during weekend breaks and arranged accommodation in Rome and Amsterdam, two European cities I had always wanted to visit. These small trips were crucial to test out my travel future. In the hostels where I stayed, I met many free spirit travelers who had been on the road for a long time. They inspired me to consider taking even longer trips and further fanned the flames of my passion to see the world. After returning to London, nothing was the same and my plans started taking shape.

Inspired by my first successful trips, I began to feel free to make bold choices for future destinations. One day, I joined the crowd at the Cuban carnival on the Thames River. There I encountered the experience of salsa dancing for the first time in my life and was captivated by its magic. People were dancing together to the lively music, smiling at each other and having a great time without the need for drugs or excessive alcohol. I felt a surge of joy within me, something I hadn't noticed for a very long time. This was the human affection I was looking for. It felt warm and connecting and genuine.

I soon decided to holiday on my own for two weeks in Cuba. It was another major milestone on my path to taking the final leap to becoming a full-time world traveler. My vacation was a stimulating mixture of backpacking on my own, dating local girls, learning to salsa dance, drinking the famous local rum and smoking Cuban cigars. I met and partied with other backpackers and felt more alive in those two weeks than I had since my arrival in the UK. It was difficult to leave the soft, tropical warmth with its vital energy but I intuitively knew I would be back to the area somehow.

When I returned to my busy London life, nothing could stop me from traveling the world. I had awakened the curiosity of my 12 year-old me who, after his first trip to Germany, wanted to know more about what existed beyond the borders of Poland. I was more than ready to begin my adventures.

The company I worked for was in the process of changing ownership and I was advised to wait to for redundancy instead of quitting. That way, I would receive an extra three months tax-free salary. It made good sense to add this money to my savings so I decided to wait. In order to keep the travel spirit alive in the interim, I bought my first SLR camera and started preparations for my future.

When I was in Havana, I met two fellow travelers, Bartek and Lukasz who inspired my purchase and who added this visual dimension to my travel plans. I bought a domain, www. filipontheroad.com, and set up my own blog to begin capturing and sharing all the important experiences that I wanted to record. Meanwhile I also booked a number of short weekend trips to Lisbon, Andalusia, Dublin, Prague, Scotland, and Copenhagen.

Through my blog, I reconnected with Thomas, the friend with whom I first traveled to the U.S. Once again, he proposed that we take a trip together for a month-long adventure to Australia and New Zealand. I was overjoyed to accept!

The life-long preparations to fulfill my dream of seeing the world were complete. From the first sparkle of desire I felt at 12 years old to my learning that I could achieve miracles through prayer to all the singular relationship events that nudged me towards stepping beyond my perceived limitations, I knew I was ready to change my life. I was already transformed by the little excursions I had taken and I was filled with excitement and anticipation of what I would learn and discover on the path that lay ahead.

PART III

PREPARATION... SMALL TRIPS BEFORE HITTING THE ROAD

2006-2007

The next series of trips continued to build my globetrotting confidence and helped me keep my dream alive while I waited to finally set foot on the road more permanently. Each new experience strengthened my commitment to world travel and uncovered a level of happiness and sense of freedom I had never known before. It was as if, with every new country I visited and with every person I encountered, a new part of myself emerged.

~

Solo Adventures In The Mediterranean

My Londoner friends were too busy to join me and my Polish friends were struggling to pay their bills so, again, I traveled on my own. I bought my flight ticket to Lisbon, Portugal and added a new Nikon d50, SLR camera to my backpacking gear.

It took me no time at all to get used to the warm, sunny February weather that was a stark contrast to the cold European winter I had just escaped. Lisbon itself was a delicious mixture of the old and new, the historic and artistic.

At the hostel in the center of the city, I was delighted to meet other backpackers from all around the world. As I listened to their travel stories and learned of their future plans, I felt the excitement rise in me. This was definitely my destiny.

They introduced me to Michael Franti who is an inspiring poet, musician, social justice activist and world traveler. His personal mission added another powerful incentive for me to travel full time. I wanted to share some part of supporting the message of love, mutual respect and compassion that he was bringing to people across the globe. For me, this was just another sign that my decision was right.

There was so much to explore in Lisbon. With the tireless energy of a child, I roamed the city and investigated its romantic, narrow streets, discovered an incredible array of art from ancient to modern and marveled at the medieval architecture of palaces and churches.

Everything was a feast for my spirit and my body. The heavy food I was used to eating at Wetherspoons in London was traded for light Mediterranean dishes that consisted of mostly seafood, fresh vegetables and wine.

I took the time to get to know the local people who, even though their English was limited, spoke to me through their warm and welcoming smiles and curious looks and gestures.

As I experimented with the functions of my new camera, I tried to capture the feel and slow pace of the Lisbon lifestyle in the random pictures I took. From the first day, I fell completely in love with street photography. There was something about it that focused my inner sight as I adjusted the camera lens on a subject. It made me realize how amazing and easily accessible the world really was.

Watching children passionately engaged in playing street football reminded me of my own similar childhood pastime. Dedication to this sport is instilled very early in this part of Europe. It is easy to see why it is such a treat to watch the teams from this area play football. Their passion and love of the game is as close to them as their own skin.

At the beach, the scent from the ocean breezes felt refreshing as I warmed my feet with the soothing touch of the sand sifting through my toes. Monstrous waves rolled onto the beach and delivered ecstatic surfers back to shore under a perfect blue sky. I walked past tanned locals as they chilled on the seaside benches. I hopped onboard an old wooden tram that precariously navigated the steep hills and old pavement of this historic city and made my way to the famed Jeronimos Monastery and its accompanying structures. I stared in amazement at the Belem Tower, a celebrated landmark built on its property in the 1500's to guard Lisbon's harbor.

Hundreds of years ago, this harbor area had been the jumping off point and the last sight of the homeland for explorers like Portugal's beloved, Vasco da Gamma. I felt a close kinship to his adventurous nature as I stood on the very ground he and the crew under his command had walked when they boarded the first ships to sail directly from Europe to India.

The long seaside hike from Lisbon to the beautiful coastal town of Cascais was inspiring. As I stood at the water's edge of this gorgeous artistic district, I knew I wanted to discover what was on the other side of this vast ocean. The unknown journeys that lay ahead of me seemed as significant and beckoning as Vasco da Gamma's must have felt to him. Even before this trip was complete, I could not wait for the next adventure to begin.

~

The Beer Drinking Culture

As I had heard good things about Dublin, my next destination was the Irish capital city. After the sunny and warm experience in Lisbon, I was met with the rain and wind of Dublin's soggy climate. Instead of finding pictures to take, the biggest challenge with my camera here was keeping it dry! This inhospitable weather prevails throughout most of the year so it is quite understandable that beer drinking is the leading social activity of this charming island.

My main intention in visiting Ireland was to experience the typical Irish lifestyle. However, I was surprised to find that wherever I went, I discovered Polish people instead. When Poland joined the European Union, there was such a large influx of Polish immigrants to Ireland that they became the country's largest minority. I ended up hitting the local pubs with some of my new Polish friends and finally got to try a real Guinness beer.

There was a precise process involved in drinking this beer. It started with pouring it into a chilled glass. Then one was required to hold the glass up to the light in order to admire the characteristic rich dark color that was topped with creamy delicate foam. This simple ritual encouraged me to drink more because, of course, I needed to practice!

I took a tour of the brewing process at an attraction called the Guinness Storehouse. It was a part of the actual brewery built by Arthur Guinness in 1759 that was open to the public and featured interactive displays and tasting rooms.

I discovered just why this stout, as it is called, is so unique and the product purchased in Ireland is the only true version of it available in the world. The barley used in the production is grown only in Ireland. Its yeast ingredient originated in the early 1800's and in order to maintain the precise consistency of the flavor, has been transferred to each subsequent batch of the brew since then. For security, a sample of this is stored in a locked safe.

Beer lovers say that Ireland is the only real place to experience the authentic version of this famous frothy, dark amber brew and after visiting the facility where it is made, I agree that there is bit of magic and history in every glass of this famous brand.

Similar to England, a pub in Ireland is a loud, friendly, warm social meeting spot. The corner pub is a place where social classes disappear and lively discussions include the latest politics, financial issues or the most recent football trades and activities. It is a substitute home where everyone is invited and treated equally while being served a fresh pint of brew. Sipping a pint is the common denominator. Working class plumbers mingle easily with the CEOs of globally recognized companies. The more alcohol that is served, the livelier the atmosphere becomes.

In one of my pub encounters, I met an English couple with whom I shared my travel plans. They suggested that it would be a great idea for me to make a short movie about the traditions of people kissing as I traveled around the world. I thought it was a creative concept but it seemed a little bit too bold for me, so I did not give it another thought. Years later, I discovered that someone else had made a documentary about that very subject and the video had gone viral.

AWAKENING INSIGHT

Good ideas and inspiration are always being made available to anyone who is open to hearing about them. If it happens to you, act on the opportunity. Do not wait for the perfect moment.

Although social drinking does not ever solve any problems, the warm glow of an Irish pub does help Dubliners forget the dreary weather for a while. It provides a respite from the boredom of work and the sense of isolation that the island engenders. For me, it was a good place to practice English and meet locals. On this trip, I realized that my beer drinking had become a habitual way to meet people and strike up a conversation. I realized that fact more clearly in Dublin but it was my preferred method to connect in London as well.

Although Dublin was fun, it was not a place that resonated with my soul. That said, it did give me an important piece of information about habits and how they form. It was a small nugget of wisdom for me to notice and remember for the future.

~

Worldcup At The Square

In the summer of 2006, I visited Prague, the capital of the Czech Republic. The three things I loved most about this country were the light brew, the dark humor and the Czech language, which sounded like an intriguingly twisty version of Polish.

I had arranged to meet one of my best mates, Kowik in Prague. Our goal was pretty simple: watch the FIFA World Cup that was taking place in Germany, drink local lager and have as much fun as possible by joining the impassioned crowd of avid football fans.

We spent our days in the main square of hot and sunny Prague watching the World Cup series and cheering for different teams. At night, we became amateur filmmakers. Armed with our handycam, we would crash the local clubs and fashion shows pretending to be journalists. Our charade garnered us interviews with local girls and provided us with regular entertainment.

The time with Kowik was a wonderful reunion not only with my good mate but also with myself. As we enjoyed exploring Prague together, I was flooded with memories of the best of times with him in our younger days in Poland. We roamed the Old Town Square, explored the famous Prague Castle and crossed the Charles Bridge as we talked and laughed at the private jokes only we understood. We eventually returned to the hostel exhausted but comfortably at peace and grateful for the time we were fortunate to share together.

Good laughter, great company, football, friendly locals and the steamy, crowded underground nightclubs made this an unforgettable trip. Although I had to come back to rainy

London, the next trip was already in the planning stages. Before leaving the UK, I wanted to visit Scotland to participate in the famous summer celebrations in Edinburgh called, the Edinburgh Festival.

~

Edinburgh, Scotland

Street Art For Free

The festivities of the Edinburgh Festival take place over three weeks in late summer and are actually a number of smaller festivals scattered throughout the city. The celebration is dedicated to the performing arts and has been an annual event since 1947. It is considered to be one of the most important street art carnivals in the world.

The atmosphere of a city in festival mode was very appealing to me so I took full advantage of as many of the free amateur shows as I could. Theater, dance and art displays were everywhere to be enjoyed. I became especially interested in the stand-up comedy acts and loved a puppet rock band act that played the music of ACDC. It was all thoroughly entertaining and uplifting. Although I did not have a chance to meet many local people, I did have the opportunity to experience their wild sense of humor and enjoy the thick Scottish brogue of their dialogue that I heard all around me.

While walking the streets of the city, I spotted a poster announcing a live show with one of the movie heroes of my youth, Kevin Smith. The many comedic films he directed were some of my lifelong favorites and I was determined to take in his live appearance that evening.

With directions in hand, I caught a local bus to the theater but when I arrived at the ticket window, I was informed that the show was sold out. Not willing to take 'no' for an answer, I indicated I would wait and put my name on a cancellation list. I was convinced that I would get a ticket and I was right. There were some last minute cancellations that provided a space for me. I gratefully sank into the seat and thoroughly enjoyed the performance.

To me, it was no coincidence that this occurred. It was simply the result of my complete conviction that it would happen and my focused ability to imagine just that scenario. During this trip, I clearly came to understand that nothing is impossible if you dare to dream it and hold the heartfelt belief that it will manifest.

AWAKENING INSIGHT

Everything is possible if you dare to dream. The Universe is always working in the background to make your dreams come true. Notice when the event happens and appreciate the magic.

After exploring the Festival, I decided to visit Scotland's largest city, Glasgow, to check out the local nightlife there. I had heard that it was a wild yet friendly center of activity but I never expected to experience what happened to me there. At one local pub I made friends with a few amiable Scots as we enjoyed jovial conversation over drinks.

"Hi there! How's it going?" I asked, smiling at two women and a man sitting next to me at the bar.

"Good! Where are you from? "

"I am 100% Polish, exploring your beautiful Scotland! Glad to be here! " I told them with enthusiasm.

"Welcome to Scotland! There are many Polish people here. I like Poles! You guys are funny! " One of the women said as she introduced herself and her friends.

"Thank you! I like your accent. Can you teach me some words in your native language, Gaelic? "

"Sure, 'thank you' is Tapadh leat and Hi Halò. " They said laughing as I attempted to repeat the foreign words.

"Brilliant, I think I need to have a local brew to improve my pronunciation. " I said laughing as I asked for a local beer at the bar.

It was fun for me to engage people in this way and begin to learn about each place I visited. I found myself very comfortable asking questions that put others at ease around me.

I wanted to explore other pubs in the area but unfortunately picked the wrong place for the next pint. It didn't turn out to be quite as friendly as the first place. I was talking to a woman I had just met and waiting for my beer in the second tavern, when a Polish thug came out of nowhere, punched me in the face and tried to pick a fight with me. One look at his imposing size and his steroid rippled body and I realized that taking my anger and frustration out on him might not ultimately be in my best interest. I moved away and soon departed the pub and headed for the hostel. Sometimes the better part of courageous behavior is to know when to leave.

Why had this happened to me? Out of all the other people in that establishment, why did this guy pick on me? I had to admit that I was looking for excitement and action and began to wonder if perhaps I was subconsciously drawn to pick places where unexpected and unusual events were sure to unfold. Could it be that my energy and desire for adventure had actually pulled me toward a similar field of vibration in the form of the goon who hit me?

As difficult as that was for me to accept, I had learned enough from the Law of Attraction material to see its principles at work in the events of the past few days. During my trip to Scotland, the attractor factor had delivered to me both a glorious experience of attending a performance I wanted to see and an unwanted physical attack. If I remained unaware of its power in my life it could be either a powerful tool or a potential minefield of trouble. This was only the beginning of my learning about working with its power.

~

So Many Reasons To Learn Spanish

I missed the Mediterranean lifestyle and with my fifth airline ticket to Spain in hand, I was on the next available flight to Andalusia. I had fallen madly in love with this country and its famous sunny year round weather. There were the inviting beaches that lined the Mediterranean waters and stretched for miles; its fascinating cities where everything was vibrant and alive; the palm trees that blended into the sun and sky and cast dancing shadows on the Old World architecture of the city center squares and, of course, its colorful culture and passionate, sensual people.

There was everything to like about Spain. It boasted great football with enthusiastic fans. It offered healthy foods such as the local tapas dishes and provided cheap, good wine (an added bonus to the travel experience!). Although only few Spaniards spoke English, especially in the southern coastal Andalusian region, I still managed to meet and interact comfortably with many welcoming and warm locals. Although I didn't understand what was being said, I loved the seductive sound of the Spanish language and I promised myself I would learn to speak it one day.

I met with Kowik in Cadiz, a port city in the southwest of Spain and one of oldest locales in Southwestern Europe. Kowik and I moved from one lazy town to another taking local transportation and making a few short stops along the way.

We arrived at the tiny seaside village of Punta Umbria and caused quite a stir among the locals at a pub. Apparently tourists were not a common sight as the town was off the beaten path. After sharing the local fare of prawns and beer with the pub patrons, we took pictures with everyone and enjoyed a wonderful few hours. We found a place to stay, had a good night's sleep and were on the road again in the early morning.

The next night, we slept in a tent on the beach of Los Caños and were lulled to sleep by the rhythmic sound of the Mediterranean waves washing ashore. We woke to the sweet laughter of the Madrilenian women who had pitched a tent next to ours. As we cleared the sand out of our hair, we prepared to begin the day with a lighthearted sense of enthusiasm. We played frisbee on the beach, swam in the sea at will and generally enjoyed life as it was meant to be lived.

Traveling in Spain, Portugal and soon in Italy demonstrated to me how much our wellbeing depends on a sincere smile and human affection. It warmed my heart to spot a happy old man on the beach or engage with cheerful children spontaneously posing for my camera. Big family gatherings where everyone ate dinner in their backyards were a common occurrence and an excuse to share good times in the tranquility of a warm evening under a night sky filled to the brim with stars.

I always felt welcome and at home in Latin cultures. Perhaps it had a lot to do with the temperate weather and the quantity of sunny days but people in these countries valued a slow lifestyle, family bonds and genuine friendship. Whatever the reason, I was never more at ease and in joy than I was when I spent time there.

AWAKENING INSIGHT
Wellbeing depends on a sincere smile and the ability to open to the warmth of authentic human affection.

Forty Days And Thousands Of Miles

While I was waiting to be declared redundant from work, one of my old friends from University, Thomas, with whom I had traveled to the U.S. the first time, made good on his earlier invitation to join him and his companions on their trip to Australia and New Zealand.

November was a particularly depressing time of year to be living in Europe. The cold, rainy climate and the absence of sun only added to my growing desire to feel the presence of human affection in my life again. The prospect of a trip to explore another hemisphere where summer was in bloom seemed like a great and timely idea.

Thus began my forty-day tour through the Land Down Under with Thomas and three other Polish friends. I left dark, dreary London and arrived in the light and warmth of summer in Sydney, Australia.

Australia/Oceania was a land of stark contrast between its modern cities of metal and glass that stood against the backdrop of the primal rock formations and the fiery orange desert sand of the Outback. Its urban dwellers seemed happy, healthy and friendly in their clean, well-organized cities that were quite westernized and bustled with activity. The tiny villages of the Outback offered a considerably slower pace with less focus on time and busyness. The people seemed more relaxed, open to listening and gave the impression they would easily extend a helping hand to others.

We toured as many of the country's attractions as we could possibly squeeze into our schedule. The whole trip had been planned by my friends and left no free time for spontaneous exploring. I realized very early on that I had accepted the invitation to travel with them without knowing their traveling style.

They wanted to sightsee and were on a mission to visit every attraction they had penned into the itinerary. What was most important to me was having the freedom to seek adventure and go with the flow as I had done on my solo trips to Cuba and Spain. But this time, I was dependent on them so I went along with the structured plan even though it was not my preferred method of travel.

Our accelerated motoring looped us through the island of Tasmania, a magical, unspoiled environment wild with dark, tropical forests, craggy mountains, lush valleys and silent, mystical places. We visited a lake fringed with fallen, moss covered trees whose massive roots exposed at the water's edge seemed silent testimony to the presence of an ancient untold tale. It could easily have been a setting from "Lord of the Rings".

As quickly as we had entered the enchanting world of Tasmania, we departed it and were on to the Great Ocean Road, considered to be one of the most spectacular scenic tourist attractions in Southeastern Australia. From the expansive, uninhabited beaches that fringed the crystal clear ocean water to the tropical green forests teeming with wildlife, the landscape provided an impressive variety of nature's best.

From the Great Ocean Road, we entered the Outback on our way to Uluru also known as Ayers Rock. Because our itinerary was so jam-packed, we sometimes had to drive at night to get everything in. These nocturnal excursions were not without their gifts. We had stopped in the darkness on the road to our Uluru/Ayers Rock destination. Standing on the desert road, I happened to look up and was met with a most magical night sky staring back at me. It was filled with bright twinkling stars and felt as close to me as the dome of stars in an observatory. I grabbed my sleeping bag from the campervan, lay down outside under this silent vastness and contemplated the beauty and mystery of this infinite universe of which I was a part. Where do we come from and where are we going? What is our purpose?

AWAKENING INSIGHT

Where do we come from and where are we going?
These are significant questions to ask about life.
Take the time to reflect on them.

When we arrived at Uluru, we only took a few pictures before we had to head off to our next destination. I intuitively sensed there was a deep meaning and magic hidden in the area. But sadly, there was little time to experience the spiritual aspects of the area or soak in the energy of the place.

Our next stop was the Great Barrier Reef where I enjoyed a most amazing snorkeling trip on Whitsunday Island. I had never seen anything quite like the coral gardens in this silent underwater world. The showy profusion of vivid colors and unexpected shapes were breathtaking images I will never forget.

On our return to Sydney, my friends decided to make a side trip to the nearby city of Adelaide. I chose to stay and explore the world famous Bondi Beach in Sydney's suburbs. We split up for a day and agreed to meet back in Sydney. The day was a relief as I fully embraced a rare moment of freedom and tried my hand at learning to surf. I struggled to even stand up on the surfboard but had great fun participating in a local passion.

From Sydney, we proceeded to Melbourne where we roamed the streets, admired the unique and attractive street art displays of wall murals, stencils and paste-ups. I was inclined to stop at some of the inviting small cafes along the way to spend time with the locals and sample the fare but there was always the issue of the plan, which took precedence over anything else.

With such an intense pace, our little group had its ups and downs. Five people in the close quarters of a vehicle can naturally ignite tension. After the first week we started petty arguments over space in the fridge and whose feet smelled the worst. We could not agree on who was driving next or even where we had to go to follow our plan. Despite these heated moments, overall, we got along quite well. When we did take the time to stop, we were often filled with awe and wonder at the beauty we witnessed.

The possibility of doing this as a full-time experience was becoming more real by the day. Even with the conflict of travel styles that was a daily obstacle, I was absolutely over my London blues and felt a deep sense of satisfaction at being on the road. There was so much of this exquisite world to see. If this less than ideal trip affected me so positively then I could see how much pleasure and excitement a worldwide tour might deliver. All I needed to do was to dare take the step and leave the security of my London life and all it represented.

I was more convinced than ever as a result of this jaunt that solo travel was my personal preference. In order to see the world on my terms, it was going to have to be accomplished alone.

As unforgettable as some of the more amazing sites we took in were, even this Australian paradise had its dark side. There were the sad images of drunken Aborigines, the native Australians, begging for money at gas stations. Their beautiful mystical culture that was based on the concept of using dreams as guidance and living in harmony with nature had been destroyed. This once proud people had been marginalized in the same way that the North American Indians were cast aside.

Although there were government sponsored social programs to help them re-cultivate their unique culture, too much damage had been inflicted in the past to reverse its effects. In witnessing this tragedy in Australia, I felt the deepest compassion for the plight of indigenous people globally. For the first time I was not proud of my European heritage.

At the time I did not understand the problem from the broader perspective. I didn't see that European aggression had been motivated by their struggle for survival. I did not understand that these invasions, as brutal and painful as they were, also had positive outcomes that expanded the learning and progress of humanity overall. On the other hand there was value in native cultures that taught us about the power of nature and its healing potential. They showed us how to live in harmony with our environment and not destroy it.

However, at that time, I did not perceive these events as the invisible forces of the Universe influencing the interactions of our global cultures and our human evolution. I only saw the immediate effects of devastation and suffering at the hands of the ignorance of others.

I had also been disheartened to see tourists climbing the sacred mountain of Uluru even though it was forbidden. Their blatant disrespect of native traditions for the sake of a picture spoke volumes of the insensitivity that I often noticed. I continued on my journey a little less lighthearted but with greater awareness of the more grim aspects of humanity.

~

Australia, New Zealand
"All the freaky people make the beauty of this world"

Sheep And Hills

New Zealand is Australia's younger sibling. It is quieter, cleaner, more polite and in some ways, more predictable. It is also more rural in its approach to life. There is a standard joke that New Zealand has more sheep than it has people or Kiwis as the population are often called.

Because we moved so fast from the south to the north island of the country we were unable to fully experience any local lifestyle or really grasp much of the culture. We did take in the ever-present stunning scenery of the two magnificent islands surrounded by the pristine ocean waters. It did not surprise me that New Zealand was a paradise for nature and extreme sport lovers.

I finally managed to convince my friends to make a stop at the legendary Black Water Rafting (cave tubing) attraction in the Waitomo Caves. This expertly guided activity rappels participants, Indiana Jones style, into the darkness that is the ancient Ruakuri caves. It then begins a heartpounding underground tubing adventure over waterfalls and into serene pools that eventually exits the cave at the end of the trip. While in the cave, resident fluorescent glowworms put on a spectacular light show overhead on the limestone cave walls.

Our visit to New Zealand was enriched with a boat tour around the fiords, picture taking moments with penguins and trekking hikes to the massive glacier on the south island. We witnessed Rotorua's hot springs and geysers whose magnificence and mystery can easily compete with Yellowstone in the category of bizarre nature. At day's end, we slept in a jail that had been transformed into the local youth hostel.

In contrast to the tragic Aborigines' challenges in Australia, New Zealand's Maori native culture was surprisingly alive and fully respected in the country. Its people participate in all activities with little fanfare and total acceptance. To an outsider such as myself however, it was both curious and uplifting to watch Maori with their fully tattooed magnificent faces standing before a crowd singing pop songs at a karaoke bar.

I left New Zealand with a deep regard for this country's ability to evolve its multi-cultural history and Polynesian connections. It showed me something about awakening to my own heritage that had sensitized me to the hardships of others.

Upon my return to England, I noticed that I held little of the original inner despair that had started the journey. The answers to my questions about my identity had begun to appear in the unspeakable magic of the starry nights, the magnificent beauty of the coral gardens, the incredible excitement of the cave tubing and especially in the heartbreaking visions of the natives lost and alone in their own country. In a way, the dark and the light I had experienced on this journey was instrumental in taking another step toward my own growth and self-knowledge. I did not realize it consciously however. All I wanted to do was travel and discover more about the world.

At that time, I did not know that learning more about the world would always teach me more about what was buried inside me that I needed to see. I was unaware that the answers to the many questions about love and life and God that I had wondered about for such a long time would be shown to me in my adventures on the road.

I began my preparations for the lifestyle change of permanent travel thinking only of the physical journey that was about to begin.

~

Back To England - Last Month

My last month in London was spent waiting for the redundancy to occur. I continued improving my photography skills by taking many pictures and I socialized with my friends who I would soon be leaving.

Since the beginning of 2007, I had been constantly bothered by phone calls from investment experts offering me cheap mortgages. No matter how many times I explained I was not interested in purchasing a home and that I had plans to travel, they did not give up. Many of my workmates were on their second or third mortgages and I was often encouraged by them to follow their lead. But I did not alter my course.

I stood against all advice and refused to participate.

I did not want to become enslaved to a bank or to be manipulated by the greed of real estate brokers hungry for profit. I wanted to travel. That was my goal and my dream and this loyalty to myself saved me the losses suffered by many in the financial catastrophe of 2008.

At one time, I had read a book entitled, "Whatever you Think, Think the Opposite" by global marketing guru, Paul Arden that encouraged my independent thinking. Practicing limited exposure to the influences of mass media's news and advertising as suggested by Tim Ferriss in "The 4-Hour Work Week" also helped me gain confidence in my own decisions no matter what others were saying or doing. It seemed the even in these experiences, there was a quiet guidance clearing the way for my dream to become a reality.

AWAKENING INSIGHT
*Have the personal confidence and inner strength
to listen to your heart and trust in yourself, no
matter what others think you should do.*

SYNCHRONICITY - HOW PAST ACTIVITIES AFFECT CURRENT EVENTS

*"Coincidences are not accidents but signals from the
universe which can guide us toward our true destiny"*
~Deepak Chopra

A few months before I hit the road, I received an unsolicited response to some comedy movies I had published and promoted on YouTube and on a private website. I did not know the person but was intrigued by his message:

"Hi! My name is Bartek. I live in London and I am also from Gdansk. I enjoyed watching the comedy movies you and your Polish friend made. If you have time I would like to meet you and have a chat"*

* Between 2002-2006, my best friends from Poland and I produced and edited a series of amateur short movies. We called them "Night in the 3city". We would dress in themed costumes, attend a number of parties and film people's antics and responses to our unusual attire. The first movie in this series was inspired by the hilarious skit from "Saturday Night Live", which was entitled "The Roxbury Guys". The second one was a parody on gangster movies from the seventies, the third one was entitled "Afro Party and Kung-Fu" and the last one titled "Disco-Polo" was intended to poke fun at Polish popular music.

I arranged to meet Bartek and one of his friends, Rudy that same day. We instantly became friends and have maintained our connection since then. The three of us collaborated on creating a character we called Emigrobot. Rudy designed the robot outfit, I initially wore the costume and Bartek filmed me as Emigrobot performing street dances in London. It received an amazing amount of attention and publicity mainly in the UK Polish media.

AWAKENING INSIGHT
Never doubt that things happen for a reason including the people you meet on your path. The key is to pay attention and be curious about coincidences.

My new friendships led me to meet another Pole, Rywin, who was the founder of londoneyetv.com, an online video program focused on Polish cultural events in the UK. He was looking for somebody outgoing and personable to conduct interviews with famous Polish artists coming to perform in London. My Emigrobot fame along with my popular blog prompted him to hire me for the position even though I had no experience or journalism education. I met many interesting people through this connection and by June 2007, in my last few months in London, my social life had blossomed so dramatically that I momentarily considered postponing my departure.

I had been dating someone special and was about to fall in love again. I was making good money and my community was growing rapidly. The company I worked for wanted me to stay and added some lucrative incentives to keep me. They offered me a new high-paid position with the new company. As well the redundancy with a cash payout option was still available. I had to decide what to do. I knew if I didn't leave now I would not leave at all.

My boss at that time, Ashley*, advised me to go but not for more than for half a year. That way I could come back and continue working without having an unexplained gap in my resume's work history. I knew I was running the risk of ruining my professional career but I also understood at a deeper level there must be something else waiting for me. As much as I was tempted to stay, I was compelled to leave.

* I was lucky to have great bosses in my life and Ashley was no different. We laughed a lot at work and even though it was clear that he was my manager, he treated me and everyone else as equals. Maybe that is why our team was considered to be so very successful. I liked Ash a lot but chose to ignore his advice about not taking too much time off and also his suggestion to invest in a house. Before I left London, Ashley had moved on to work at a media company. In 2010 while in Colombia, I received the sad message that he had died.

The three years I lived in London expanded my consciousness and helped shift my view of what was possible. Because I had actually taken some preliminary small steps, I discovered without a doubt that exploring the world was much easier than I previously thought.

For many of my friends, London became a mental and emotional trap that made it difficult to escape. The city's attractions, unique lifestyle and its status as the center of the world were very seductive. London also boasted an amazing cultural mix, which added to its fascination. The diverse faces, language and dress were part of the mosaic that was an everyday reality on the streets of London. International influence was everywhere – in advertising, in museums, art exhibitions and in the wonderfully varied cuisine.

Thanks to my life in London I was able to immerse myself in an experience of meeting people from various backgrounds and realize how comfortable and authentic I felt when I was engaged in such interactions. Living in London had provided me the necessary time I needed to find what was really important to me. It gave me the opportunity to develop life skills and make enough money to finance the next inevitable step - to hit the road, explore new cultures, meet different people and discover the mysteries of life.

PART IV

ON THE ROAD... WISDOM AND SPIRITUAL AWAKENING

JUNE 2007 – JUNE 2008

"There is only one way to learn. It's through action. Everything you need to know you have learned through your journey."
~ Paulo Coelho, The Alchemist

Being Flexible

A few weeks before leaving London, I had to change my itinerary. I received a message that my cousin and a very close friend were both getting married in August in Poland.

My original travel plans had me in Asia at that time so I decided to start my trip in northern Italy then visit Eastern Europe, attend the weddings in Poland and move on to Asia. The Eastern European leg of the trip did not hold a great attraction for me as the cultures and history were the same as my native Poland but, given the circumstances, I decided to be flexible and open-minded. After all, my new life was about discovery and it could be an opportunity to get to know this part of the world in a new way.

With no job responsibilities, summer time was a perfect time to enjoy my new freedom. It had been a long time since I was able to be completely carefree and I was ready to live in the moment, absorb the reality of being on the road and have as much fun as I possibly could.

I found a cheap flight from London to Pisa, Italy and took the first step into my new life. It was exhilarating to know this was not a vacation but my *actual life* now. I could barely contain my excitement.

Warm Human Relationships

In the few short hours I spent in Pisa, I knew why I was traveling. Seeing the spectacular Leaning Tower was not the only highlight in the city. It was a visual, orgasmic delight to be among the warmth, the smiles and the embraces of people on the street. It had been a long time since I had seen such public displays of affection that were so genuine. I could not take my eyes off the beautiful women as they passed by, their sensual summer dresses floating around their swaying bodies. This was life I wanted.

Satisfied and content, I moved on to Florence, where I stayed for few days at an apartment I found through the Couchsurfing website. Thanks to this travel community network, I was able to stay in Florence for free.

It was the first night of my new life and I started it in style. Through the Couchsurfing recommendations, I met Dominika and spent a wonderful time with her as my host and guide. She was studying international relationships abroad on the student exchange program, Erasmus, and had made many connections in the Florentine culture.

Dominika knew a bartender who worked at Cavali, one of the trendiest bars in Florence. She took other Couchsurfers and myself to a party there where we drank expensive liquor at discount prices and relaxed in the VIP lounge surrounded by beautiful women. That night she introduced me to people from all over the world including Maciek, a Polish medical student who was my first on the road contact. We stayed in touch and two years later, I visited him in Sao Paulo, Brazil.

AWAKENING INSIGHT
If you feel lonely and disconnected where you live, find a place where you can meet people who share similar values to yours.

Living Museum

Florence has been ranked as one of the most beautiful cities on the planet. It has a fascinating and turbulent history as the center of trade and commerce in medieval Europe. Once ruled by the powerful and wealthy Medici family who were patrons of the arts, Florence is testament to their legacy as it probably has more art and stunning architecture per square foot than any other city in the world.

Instead of taking a guided tour, I decided to sightsee on my own, spontaneously walking wherever the map took me, discovering places without knowing about their origin and historical importance. I explored churches, museums and galleries such as the Uffizi and the Palazzo Pitti that were housed in palaces built in the 1500's. Evidence of the city's rich and creative past was everywhere. The awe-inspiring works of Michelangelo, Botticelli and DaVinci were on the frescoed walls of the churches and in the statues that adorned the narrow streets, courtyards and fountains that I passed on my outing. There was more to see than I had the energy for. Soon my legs were aching and I was ready to rest.

The next day, after a refreshing night's sleep, I was on my way to Venice. An Australian woman sat beside me on the bus. She seemed less than impressed with my Bondi Beach, Australia t-shirt that I showed her as I tried to strike up a conversation. She put earplugs in and simply ignored me while she pretended to intently read her travel guide. I realized that despite my consistent enthusiasm to get to know everyone I could, not all fellow travelers are created equal. Sometimes there is no connection. I spent the rest of the trip watching the countryside pass by and focused on the wonders of Venice that lay ahead.

Venice, London
"What is love?"

Love And The Scent Of Venice At The Pier

Each time I visited Italy it felt more and more like home. Each of the cities I had already traveled to – Palermo in Sicily, Rome and Milan – had its own unique and memorable experiences that left me wanting more but nothing prepared me for the heart-stopping beauty and romance of Venice.

The ambience of the city awakened the senses. No matter where I looked, enchanting palaces, basilicas and art galleries rose up before me.

I watched as gondolas drifted down the Grand Canal past the sun-drenched stucco structures and charming shops and cafes. I crossed the canal on foot over The Rialto, one of the many bridges that spanned the waterway. Built in the late 1500's, this bridge is one of the city's main tourist attractions. The city was an endless display of spectacular architecture.

I inhaled the sweet scent of the sea breezes mixed with the inviting aroma of basil, sun dried tomatoes, mozzarella and fresh pizza that poured from the restaurants. The margaritas and pizza were so fresh and delicious that I have never again tasted anything that comes close to their perfection.

As I walked along the street, I was completely swallowed up by the sensual romance of it all. I noticed a beautiful woman standing in front of a church and decided to get to know her.

"Excuse me, do you know any place for a cheap local pizza around?" I really could have cared less about where the pizza was but it was a good way to start small talk.

"I do not know. I am not from here." She looked quite interested in continuing the conversation however.

"Oh, I am sorry, my name is Filip, and I am from Poland. Nice to meet you." I said

She seemed friendly as she introduced herself and her friend who was just coming out of the church.

"Hi Filip. My name is Ana and this is my friend Paula. We are from Argentina."

I invited them for a glass of wine and. we spent a lovely time together.

"I have not met many people from Argentina yet. Tell me about your country and what brought to Italy?" I felt like I had joined in the romance of the city as we engaged in conversation and became acquainted. I was interested and excited to listen to the stories about the unknown world that I would soon be exploring.

Eventually, it was time to say goodbye. As we parted, I promised to visit them on my planned visit to their country. I continued on with my dreamy explorations of Venice.

I watched as a young man proposed to a woman on one of the nearby bridges. Everywhere couples were holding hands, laughing together and sharing delicious local food. It was easy for me to forget I was a tourist as I melted into the culture and absorbed the joy and love that was all around me.

I made my way to a wooden pier by the canal and sat down as people passed by. An aroma of wet wood rose up from the pier and mixed with the softness of the day and the uplifting energy of the scene before me. I was reminded of the powerful feeling of love and all the warm human relationships I had known in Poland. I realized that my life had become so focused on my career and work when I was in London that I had lost touch with this part of my being. It felt good to be surrounded by people who genuinely enjoyed their life and took time to celebrate it.

AWAKENING INSIGHT

*In Venice, take the time to sit down on the wooden pier and
observe the smiling couples crossing one of the many bridges.
Be truly happy for all that is before you.*

Welcome To The Eastern Europe

After spending a few days in Italy, I moved on to nearby Slovenia and its political, economic and cultural capital city, Ljubljana. Ljubliana was my first stop in the trip across the Eastern Europe. Even though delicious pizzas were replaced by Eastern European fried street foods, I found it very interesting to travel across countries that I had not initially planned to visit.

Eastern Europeans bear the scars and the gifts of their violent and destructive Communist occupation from 1945 to 1989. Although they may be behind their Western European neighbors economically and may be a bit less confident, they have learned to be hardworking, humble and flexible. They know what it takes to survive and will invest the effort and time it takes to reach their ultimate goals. They are eager to learn and pick up any new skills quickly. I know many graduates with master's degrees who work abroad as construction workers, waiters and bartenders while they continue to look for work in their field of education.

Because of their history, Eastern Europeans are more resilient in response to the ups and downs of financial uncertainty. Those who remember the hardships of extreme inflation from the old system usually avoid the trap of credit debt. They know how to save money and support their families.

Although I have spent years seeking my identity and struggling with the intolerance of others because of my nationality, I must admit that I am happy that I was born in Poland. The influence of its culture has made me strong, adaptable and very grateful for whom I have become.

Student Parties And Fun

Ljubljana is a city whose origins date back to 2000 BC and whose long history is checkered with numerous territorial skirmishes, ethnic conquerors, earthquakes, destructive fire and several reconstructions.

Modern Ljubljana is a thriving city of galleries, industry and education. Its preserved Old Town city center becomes a hub of social activity in the summertime with cafes, bars and street entertainment spilling onto the small bridges that cross the Ljubljanica River that flows through the city. Ljubljana is also home to a sizeable university student population and a vital alternative lifestyle center, Metelkova.

As soon as I arrived, I found the hostel, dropped my backpack and headed out on foot to explore. The language here had that same unusual Polish slang sound that I noticed in the Czech Republic. The street food was similar to Polish cuisine, the women were attractive and the people I met were fun loving and always ready to socialize.

At night Ljubljana turned into a student party town where live music from the various underground bars mixed with the lively conversations in the streets. It felt like I had entered one of underground cinema director, Emir Kusturica's avant-garde films.

My last day in Ljubljana, a few of my hostel mates and I went out to the student's club where we partied until dawn. I met some local women who drove me around in their car while we listened to Red Hot Chili Peppers. Driving in a convertible on the open road felt as if I was living one of the rock band's videos. The wild sense of adventure and freedom that their music evoked was pulsed through every cell of my body. It was simply a *perfect* moment of *perfect* freedom and bliss and well worth the little sleep I got before leaving on the bus for Croatia the next day.

I really wanted to stay longer in Ljubljana to see what other people I might meet and what other spontaneous experiences might come my way. But I felt I had to follow my plans, especially if I was to be in Poland for the weddings I had agreed to attend. I realize now that I didn't have to be that rigid about my itinerary.

AWAKENING INSIGHT
"A good traveler has no fixed plans
and is not intent on arriving."
~ Lao Tzu

Sunsets And Trapped By Expectations

Coming from Slovenia, a sister country to Croatia, I had high expectations of a similar fun experience. Of course, this is a typical mistake every traveler makes at the beginning of his/her journey.

Croatia's coastal region on the eastern shores of the Adriatic Sea is a popular vacation destination especially in the summer when tourists flock to the exquisite beaches, perfect weather, gorgeous cities and affordable prices. Split, the second largest city in the country is located on a peninsula that juts out into the Adriatic. It is the jumping off point for access to the thousands of surrounding islands.

Split is also one of the oldest cities in Croatia. Its main historical attraction, the Diocletian Palace, was built 1700 years ago and its presence is a reminder of the ancient roots of this city. Although I admired the architecture and explored the sites of Split, I did not feel any special connection to it.

When I arrived, I felt like just another visitor in the midst of millions of tourists that descend upon the city annually. The locals generally showed little interest in the steady flow of the foreigners who seemed to become part of the background of their everyday lives.

For me, a key part of any trip was the people I met and the connections I built with them. Of course I wanted to visit the highlights of each place, walk the city streets, swim in the oceans and trek the mountains but what I wanted more was to explore new cultures and meet the locals and other traveling free spirits. I was thirsty for long conversations about life, the

Universe and was interested in understanding global issues from different perspectives.

None of these opportunities presented themselves in the throng of visitors of which I was just another one. It didn't seem that I would find any meaningful connections in Split.

Love Moments On The Road

I met Marijana on the boat that took me to the island of Hvar and finally had an opportunity to experience the special moments I had been missing. We were sitting back to back on the same bench and were both listening to Buddha Bar Chill Out music while silently observing the waves on the horizon and enjoying the pleasant Adriatic breezes.

We struck up a pleasant conversation. She was born in Germany but her roots were proudly in Croatia. She worked as a manager at an international hotel on Hvar and was very grateful for the opportunity to work in her true Croat homeland.

We soon arrived in Hvar. This island is the crown jewel of the Adriatic islands and one of the most beautiful locations in the region. We were met with the intoxicating scent from the island's abundant crops of lavender, rosemary and olives. Marijana went to work and I headed for the exquisite island beaches to do some snorkeling.

The pristine waters of Hvar's reefs offered a refreshing underwater experience and added to the magic of my day. After snorkeling, I did not go to visit Marijana as I had promised I would. In fact, I never saw her again. We were mutually attracted to each other and I felt the pull of possibility in our meeting but I was reluctant to start any relationship so soon into my journey. My priorities were about travel and I was committed to my trip.

In the short time since I had started my journey, it had been easy to engage in romantic conversations with women and feel momentary connections like I had with Marijana. I welcomed the freedom to do this. When I worked in London, I had to maintain a professional, more distant mask and it became my identity after a while. I had to act a certain way in order to fit in and thrive.

Traveling solo was an entirely different story. 1 soon discovered that I could be myself completely. I could be with whomever I wanted, which in my case, was mostly the locals. I could party if I liked or quietly watch a sunset. I began to feel relaxed and comfortable with the freedom to be me. Suddenly, it didn't matter if I was accepted by fellow travelers from the West or if everyone I met understood me. Sometimes I paid the price for my own authenticity in loneliness but it was worth it. Without even realizing it, my choice to travel had opened a door into discovering who I truly was and it showed in the heartfelt connections I had already made. There was so much more on my path.

AWAKENING INSIGHT
"Be yourself; everyone else is already taken."
~ Oscar Wilde

Do Not Judge A Book By Its Cover

After Hvar, I made my way to Dubrovnik, which was considered to be one of the most beautiful cities in Southern Europe. Besides being a busy seaport, it was a prime tourist destination that offered the sparkling beauty of the Adriatic Sea for a playground. Its medieval history lived on in the walled-in Old Town section that was one of the must see sites of its kind in the world. In Old Town, the marble streets were open only to foot traffic, which added to the charm and realism of this historic area.

Finding an inexpensive hostel online was difficult. As a novice traveler, I did not want to be without a place to stay so I had reluctantly booked accommodation at an expensive shared dormitory. It turned out to be nothing better than a made-over hostel that reminded me of the typical concrete Communist designed neighborhoods from my childhood in Poland. Situated in a residential area with similar buildings all around it, the dormitory was five floors of concrete ugly. I quickly learned, however, that even an overpriced hostel could turn into a great meeting spot. I became friends with many fellow travelers and reconnected with some of them on future trips.

One of the most interesting people I met was a woman named Kaz, from California who became my travel mate in Montenegro and who also visited me in Poland. When I went to San Francisco, she was my host there as well.

Thanks to Kaz I also met another Californian, Sheila who was my host in Venice Beach near Los Angeles. I also met a Norwegian man, Holgar, who had studied at Harvard with

Marc Zuckerberg, the founder of Facebook. Holgar told me stories about Zuckerberg and his passionate pursuits that were well known at Harvard but were never made public.

One night, my new friends and I decided to go to the beach. While they sat sharing small talk on the shore, I chose to experience a night swim in the sea. I floated on my back, supported in the embrace of the water and observed the shimmering heavens above. I was hushed into silence at the beauty and wonder of the moment that had been created. It was a memory I will always carry with me.

Sometimes it is worth it to pay more and receive the unexpected gifts that lay hidden in such a travel experience. I was grateful for the decision I made to stay at the Dubrovnik dormitory. Inside the 'ugly' I uncovered many treasures. You can never judge a situation by its outward appearance. If you approach every experience with an open mind, you will find the joy in it and the value it has to offer.

AWAKENING INSIGHT
Don't judge a book by its cover.
Approach every experience with curiosity and openness.

Lisbon, Mostar
"Lessons from fear"

Lessons From Fear

Kaz was a compatible travel companion whose unique perspective and good vibe appealed to me. She had studied languages at Yale and was attractive, intelligent and adventurous. After Croatia, we traveled together to Bosnia.

Situated on the border between Eastern and Western Europe, Bosnia and Herzegovina is slowly rebuilding and healing from its most recent civil war uprising in the 1990's. The country's war torn history has attracted travelers to explore and learn more about its past.

We stopped in the historic town of Mostar to see its most famous tourist attraction - the Stari Most, the famed sixteenth century Old Bridge that was recently reconstructed after its destruction during the 1990's war. Rising to a height of 24 meters, it arches across Mostar's Neretva River and is the favored location for annual summer diving competitions. Although the contests are recent, the practice itself is said to have begun as early as the mid-1600's. Only the most skilled and trained divers will attempt this risky leap into the frigid waters of the Neretva.

In a moment of bravado, I decided to give it a try but as I stood and looked down at the river, I remembered hearing a story at the Dubrovnik hostel from an Irish man who had jumped. He ended up with painful injuries because he did not know how to control his dive well enough. Fear (or maybe common sense) got the better of me as I thought about his experience.

In the interest of my own wellbeing, I chose to not jump. Some say that we are programmed from birth to respond to two types of fear: the fear of a sudden loud noise and the fear of falling down. Both experiences are real and will trigger our instinct to survive. All the other fears are merely a projection of our minds.

AWAKENING INSIGHT
There are two types of fear we should pay attention to in order to survive: the fear of a loud noise and the fear of falling down. The rest is merely a projection of the mind. The trick is to discern which fear you are feeling and respond accordingly.

It Pays To Be Tactful

Sarajevo was our next stop. This progressive capital city of Bosnia and Herzegovina is the country's largest and most important economic center. It boasts a multitude of cultures and religions but its most unique attraction is its place in the area as war memorial. Having recently suffered through four long years of siege during the Bosnian War conflict there are visible machine gun holes in wall, gates and buildings. Its inspiring victorious recovery from such devastation is the subject of a song performed by U2 and Luciano Pavrotti entitled "Miss Saravejo".

We had originally wanted to take a war tour of the city to learn about and witness the effects of the conflict but had been advised by a traveler that the tour was not worth taking and the guide was boring.

When we checked in to our hostel, we were offered the option of taking that very tour. Kaz off-handedly mentioned that we had already been informed about the tour and we weren't interested because it apparently had a boring guide. To our shock, the person who invited us on the war tour was in fact that boring guide and Kaz' comment did not land well on him. I would not have wanted to be in his shoes at that moment.

He erupted into a tirade about stupid, ignorant tourists who did not understand anything about the effects of war. He angrily rattled on that they didn't even care to learn and so on. In an attempt to calm him down, we agreed to take his tour, which turned to be one of the most awkward excursions I have ever experienced. It was funny to watch our guide. Each time he mentioned the ignorance of people and not caring about the tragic effects of war, he would point toward Kaz and glare at her. I could hardly hide my laughter as she spent the whole time looking wide-eyed with complete terror.

After the disastrous Sarajevo war tour, we continued our journey through several other Eastern European countries. There were delights, disappointments and surprises that brought the reality of solo travel more clearly into view. The original 'high' that had begun my trip in Pisa, Italy, found more balance as a result of my experiences in the next part of my trip.

The Newest European Country And Camera Magic

Sharing a similar tumultuous history of conflict and possession with its Balkan relatives, Montenegro recently became an independent country and is the EU's newest member. Its tiny size does not in any way diminish its status as one of the most pristine bio-diverse and captivatingly beautiful locations in the Balkans. Its sparkling beaches, mountain vistas, dramatic canyons, herb-scented air and friendly, warm citizens were a huge surprise. Unique from the most recent countries I had visited, it was unspoiled by massive tourism and that seemed to make all the difference.

I visited charming Kotor with Kaz after which we went our separate ways. She returned to Croatia to meet her boyfriend and I moved on alone to Budva where I attended a raucous beach party and toured the town.

Accommodations in Budva were readily offered at the train station for a reasonable price. Everywhere I went people were willing to pose for my camera. I left Montenegro with good memories and many happy, smiling faces in my pictures. My camera had been the instrument of magical connections with the locals of Montenegro and would prove to be a valuable link in my making friends along my future travels.

Time was getting shorter. If I was to be in Poland for the weddings in August, I had to finish my itinerary more quickly. I moved on to Albania, Macedonia, Bulgaria, Romania and Hungary without long stays at any place.

A Race Across Eastern Europe

I entered Albania with other travelers who were not Polish citizens. They were charged for a visa but I was pleasantly surprised to find out that, because I was a member of an ex-Soviet country, I was given one for free.

"At least being an ex-communist had some advantages." I thought ruefully.

Albania is viewed in the world as an impoverished country that has a population filled with Hollywood mafia-type characters. I was pleasantly surprised to find it was nowhere near as demonic as it had been made out to be. Its capital, Tirana was a great city that I completely enjoyed exploring. Apart from the unsavory poster of the much disliked ex-President George Bush mounted in the main square, it felt very European and cosmopolitan. Its nightclubs could easily have been in New York or Paris.

Up to this point in my travels, I had enjoyed unforgettable sites, learned to appreciate the history of the Balkans and made a few new friends. The nightlife scenes, high fashion influences from international brands and progressive approaches to life were pretty much the norm wherever I went. I had settled into a relatively comfortable, confident rhythm so far. My fun experiences had exceeded my expectations and I was quite content...until I reached Macedonia.

Within a very short time of my arrival in Skopje, Macedonia, I was ready to leave. The upbeat energy I felt from other countries quickly melted away as I was met with the unexpressive, tired looking faces of the locals whose slow paced lifestyle was not a good match for my more active travel process. I had great difficulty tolerating the long wait to buy bad tasting fast food and generally felt dragged down here. I took a few pictures and in short order, I was on the bus to Bulgaria.

Later on, I met people who claimed to have had an amazing time in Macedonia. I have since considered a revisit someday as my personal life perspectives have changed and perhaps my experience would be different as well.

I soon arrived in Bulgaria, which was known to most Polish youth of my generation as a summer travel destination. Any member of an Eastern Block/Communist country offered its working class citizens summer holiday packages for Bulgarian destinations. Because my father worked in Germany, which was outside the included area, we were not entitled to this offer. Thus, I had not ever taken advantage of this Bulgarian seaside perk as others had.

My youthful impression of Bulgaria was that it was a rather old-fashioned country where people tried desperately to keep up with Western trends. My opinions soon changed when I arrived in the small town of Veliko Tarnovo.

I met extremely friendly, humble and beautiful young people who were full of dreams and had an intense passion for life.

I went out for a drink with two Finnish roommates from the hostel. We found a local restaurant on the city's main street where we settled at a table and proceeded to order. My two companions were very blond so we definitely stood out from the crowd. As we sat enjoying the fare, we were approached by a group of smiling local young people.

"Hi, where you are from?" A teenager asked us in broken English.

"I am from Poland and they are Finnish."

He wanted to know if he and his friends could join us so they could practice speaking English.

"Of course! Yes we can practice English! Please feel free to sit with us. Are you students?" I asked them. I wanted to find out more about them and looked forward to conversation. We spent the whole day together and their curiosity and exuberance added immense lightness to my mood.

All that changed drastically the next day when I traveled to Varna, a town that was known as the party capital of Bulgaria and where I stayed with other Couchsurfers.

I was taken to a series of parties on the outskirts of the city by my host and was dragged from one party to the next with each successive celebration being worse than the one before. It was an all-night experience of enduring bad music, bad performances and trying to find my Couchsurfing host who had disappeared in all the frenzy. It wasn't until 6 a.m. that I finally met up with her and we went back to her place to get some sleep. This was one of the worst nights of my new life so far. After just one party experience, I had had enough of Bulgaria. I took a few pictures in Varna, grabbed a tasteless burger at the bus station and crossed the border into Romania.

Romania was actually worse than Bulgaria. It was probably the only country in Europe where I did not feel secure from the start. I was noticing a distinct turn to the negative in my travels at this point.

At the bus station in Brasov, a local hostel owner offered me accommodation. Her hostel was in the travel guide I used so I agreed to stay with her. She gave me directions to her place via the local bus and advised me to be careful with my belongings and not let them out of my sight. On the bus, I witnessed a brutal fight initiated by aggressive men who harassed innocent passengers and threatened to rob them. The incident shook my confidence and left me wary of exploring the city.

At the hostel, I met a French couple who were both doctors. We decided to visit a nearby restaurant together. The waiter tried to scam us into buying the most expensive meal on the menu, which we declined. The food I did order was not too appealing and shortly after eating it, I ended up with a severe bout of diarrhea. It may have been the result of this food plus the effects of the bus station fare in Bulgaria. No matter the source, I was grateful for the doctors' help. They gave me pills to relieve the pain and helped me recover. I was very sick and appreciative of their kindness.

Eventually, I improved enough to explore the castles of Transylvania and learn about the legendary, violent Vlad III, Prince of Wallachialad, also known as Dracula. As I walked around the courtyard of his palace, I could feel the intense low vibration. It made me very jittery and I was chilled to the bone.

The next day I went to Bucharest for a few hours and saw the palace of the Romanian murderer and Communist dictator, Nicholas Ceausescu. The capital was a study in black and white giving the city a dull gray pallor that cloaked the post-Communist atmosphere. There were no vivid colors evident anywhere. It partially reminded me of a black and white, sunless movie version of Paris from the seventies.

There was a great deal of darkness in Romania, which made the kindness of the strangers who helped me there seem even more noticeable and meaningful. Sometimes it is necessary to count on others to support you.

AWAKENING INSIGHT
*Being a traveler sometimes means
counting on the kindness of others. This is how
one develops the quality of heartfelt gratitude.*

Hungary was my next stop. Stretched out along the Danube River, the capital city of Budapest had its own array of architecture and natural offerings. My goal was to be a typical tourist, see the sites, bathe in one of the more than one hundred hot springs in the area and find some famous Hungarian goulash to taste. I did experience the hot springs but the goulash was nowhere to be found. It seemed strange to me that I could not find this food. It was, after all, a part of the culture. It seemed as unusual as it would be to not find pizza in Italy.

Like many of the cities I had recently visited, it was another majestic, pretty European face. But there was something missing. Somehow it lacked character, energy and passionate people. While walking around alone, I realized that what I was noticing in the city felt a lot like my own loneliness. Solo travel involved moments of feeling alone - no travel friends, no welcoming locals or people to talk to. This was one of those times. I missed having female company since Kaz and I had separated. The harder I tried to find someone to connect with, the lonelier I became. Was I attracting more loneliness to me?

As I roamed the city center, I made a casual acquaintance of an Australian woman. We spent a wonderful evening together sharing stories, friendly conversation and taking pictures. After that, we stayed in touch for a few years on Facebook but eventually lost contact.

Life on the road had its times of connection with others that were rich and wonderful and sometimes even romantic. These meetings could be short, long or endure for the rest of life. There were no rules. The key was to appreciate each encounter, savor its uniqueness and be as engaged as possible as it was happening.

AWAKENING INSIGHT
Solo travel has its share of lonely moments.
It is key to appreciate, savor and be present to the moments
of connection and engage them as fully as possible.

Weary of traveling alone in Eastern Europe, I was very happy to buy my train ticket to Vienna, Austria that would deliver me to family.

Although Austria is not welcoming to backpackers, I loved being in Vienna, thanks to the presence of my uncle who was also my godfather. He had moved there in the early 1980's. Besides not having seen him for years, being with family made me feel secure and emotionally connected. After the road, I appreciated having someone close to share thoughts and experiences with. My cousin was a gracious guide on this visit. He took me to bars and nightclubs and through him I discovered the natural sociability of the locals.

It was heartwarming to be in connection with communicative people again. I spent a wonderful day with an Austrian actress at a karaoke bar. My uncle and I wandered through the stylish part of Vienna at night stopping to listen to the free classical concerts that were the signature characteristic of the city.

I enjoyed the opportunity to spend quality time with my cousin, which was particularly important because he recently died suddenly. He was very entertaining and funny and a joy to be around. Even though he is no longer physically present on this earth, his memory lives on in this book and his light is deeply missed.

The time had finally come to return to Poland. I was excited to realize that for the next two weeks I would be home spending time with my loved ones.

AWAKENING INSIGHT
Being with family anywhere creates a sense of fitting in and belonging. Magic moments happen when I feel at home.

Backpacking In My Home Town

From Vienna I bought a flight to Poland. I was finally home for a while and eager to take part in two weddings and spend a few days with my family and friends.

I had not lived in Poland since May 2004 and I actually felt like a tourist in my own town. Seeing the familiar places of Gdansk through new eyes was like seeing it for the first time and I really began to appreciate its beauty.

What made it even more special was that Kaz joined me from Montenegro and I spent a couple of days showing her around Sopot and Gdansk before she departed for Turkey. It was a wonderful reunion with her. Later in my stay, I also guided her friend Sheila from California, who was in Eastern Europe. She returned the favor a year later when I visited her in Santa Monica in the Los Angeles area.

Partying at my best friend's wedding was very symbolic to me. I was single and my mate was now married. It was clear that our life paths had diverged. I wanted to find my happiness on the road without a specific plan or timetable. This was so different from my friend's decision. It was a completely non-traditional life I had chosen for myself, one that didn't necessarily involve the security of having anyone else to count on. I wanted new experiences and new adventures in my life and marriage was not a resolution to those strong desires.

After spending two weeks catching up with my family I was ready to go again. I remember the look in my mother's eyes as she waved goodbye to me as the bus pulled away from the station bound for Lithuania. I had no way of knowing that it would be three years before we would see each other again.

As hard as it might have been for her, she knew I needed to follow my own passions so she supported my decisions. Her love, understanding and belief in me were always in my heart. She was vitally important to me.

The road to Lithuania felt like freedom again. I was closer now to my original plan and was looking forward to setting foot on unknown territory and learning more.

Poland to Russia

It was just 267 miles from Gdansk to the Lithuanian capital, Vilnius where I planned to stay only one day.

Vilnius is a city with a chaotic history of civil war, siege and occupation mixed with periods of stability and multicultural expansion that dates back to the 1300's. With Lithuania's recent hard won independence from the Soviet Union, it has become the focus of reconstruction efforts that reminded me of many Polish cities in the nineties.

Because of its past connections with Poland, there is a significant population of Poles living in Vilnius, which made communication easier for me. In exploring, I came across an interesting piece of artistic history that got my attention when I came across two statues of revered Polish Romantic poets, Mickiewicz and Slowacki.

I was taught in literature classes that the nationality of these two "Shakespeares" was Polish. Lithuania and Poland had been united as one European country hundreds of years ago. I just now discovered that both poets were actually born in the territory of what is now Lithuania so their Polish roots are not so clear. It left me a bit confused and made me wonder if there was anything else I learned in school that was not accurate. It brought back memories of the rigid education system in Poland where we were forced to recite poems without any free interpretation.

The next stop of my itinerary was Riga, the capital city of nearby Latvia.

Riga although situated not far away from Vilnius was light years different in its feel and energy. Where Vilnius felt quiet and somewhat ordinary to my young traveling tastes, Riga was welcoming, interesting and had friendly, party-loving young people. It was a melting pot of Eastern European culture and had the feel and artistic attractiveness of Cracow.

I toured the city with Italian travelers, admired the sophisticated architecture of the old town and tasted local food that had Polish similarities. Some of the Communist statues around the city were stark reminders of the Russian influences of the past. A Latvian woman I met through Couchsurfing and I irreverently drank beer while seated at the foot of one of these Soviet Monuments. We laughed as we reminisced about the old days of Communist rule and thanked God they were over.

Apparently, things were going a bit too smoothly for me. The last night of my stay at the Riga hostel, I was bitten by bed bugs. As I headed to Estonia, my stomach looked like I had contracted a bout of eighteenth century smallpox disease. Even though the bites were unsightly, they cleared up in a couple of weeks without any problems.

On the way to my ultimate destination of Russia, I spent two days exploring Tallinn, Estonia. It is a town of many contradictions in one of the most non-religious countries in Europe and I felt its lack of spiritual interest. Its eclectic mix of architecture represented its conflicting culture quite well – medieval town center surrounded by modern glass and steel structures that peek out between severe Soviet concrete buildings. The contrasts in Tallinn were everywhere. In a place where there was little public display of affection or warmth, it was known for its sexually evocative Stag Weekends. Traditional communication was minimal yet it was the home of communication software successes Skype and KaZaA.

While walking around, I discovered a bar with a Depeche Mode theme. Since this was my favorite band in my teens, I immediately went inside to investigate. The décor was dedicated to pictures, history and facts about the band and their albums. Like my experience everywhere else however, my enthusiasm for the design was met with a few unfriendly grunts from the bartender who was not interested in my opinions at all.

I dejectedly made my way back to the hostel and got caught up in a conversation with a Canadian stockbroker who rambled on about minute details of his trade. It was a boring and emotionless subject of no interest to me so I turned my attention instead to Sabaka, the resident Russian dog. My next stop was Russia and, as I played with Sabaka, I wondered if I would find any Slavic souls like myself in the days ahead.

Typical of my heritage and culture, life was never about holding back. Life was to be lived full on with openness, honesty and passion. For me, it mattered that I could connect openly and honestly with others, that I could share my good and bad experiences. Nothing was more life giving to me than exchanges of the heart that helped me find out about someone else's life and experiences while I shared mine.

In my stays at hostels I had often experienced a familiar impersonal energy similar to what I felt when I lived in London. I saw the same western patterns, the same masks and the same distant interaction between people in hostels.

It seemed that the only way any genuine conversation took place between travelers was when alcohol lubricated the dialog. For my part, I usually found the local communities to be more compatible and authentic. Unfortunately, my experience in Tallinn, however, didn't seem to offer that local connection either.

Russia is Russia

Covering over 17 million square kilometers, Russia, besides being the largest country in the world, is a country of contrasts and diversity. Its rich culture has shared music and dance, literature, architecture and the arts internationally. The Russian Ballet, Stravinsky, Pushkin and Tolstoy, the iconic colorful, spires of Saint Basil's Cathedral in Moscow's Red Square and the famous painted Matryoshka nested dolls bear witness to Russia's influence in the world.

However, its cultural attractions hide a darker violent past of civil wars and revolutions that gave rise to Communism and oppression of its citizens. It is the home of horrific historical figures, which are ironically regarded as heroes by some Russians. Its legendary mafia with a presence throughout the world has existed since the time of the Tsarist rule. In its history, it has experienced immense political change from empirical rule to its current status of federal semi-presidential republic.

Even though it is the fifth largest economy in the world, the divide between rich and poor is drastic and obvious. On the main streets of Moscow you can see wealthy, exclusively dressed young people driving Ferraris and right around the corner you can find an old lady sell meager vegetables to other poor people as all simply try to survive.

My basic Russian learned from the Communist education system was finally of some use to me. I knew enough to help me communicate. The locals I met were friendly, usually well-educated people with a good sense of humor and were very keen to share conversation. Even their slight natural pessimism about life in general added a certain charm to my impressions of this nation.

Saint Petersburg, located on the eastern shore of the Baltic Sea, is a historical and cultural Russian treasure. Its palaces, monuments and architecture are testimony to its sophistication and artistic beauty. I took the time to visit the sprawling Hermitage Museum, which is one of the world's oldest and largest museums. It is housed in the collection of opulent palaces that were home to Russian emperors of the past. It is a breathtakingly gorgeous facility that is a not to be missed experience.

Moscow on the other hand, had a more business-like atmosphere and was also rich with historical, awe-inspiring architecture. It was not, however without access to modern bars and inviting cafes. I found a place called, Lenin Bar where I took the opportunity to try the famous Bliny's – traditional Russian buckwheat and yeast pancakes. It was a familiar taste from my high school cafeteria days. Although unhealthy, it was comfort food.

The Moscow Metro Museum was built in 1935 under Joseph Stalin as an artistic part of the city's subway system. The museum was added as a living tribute to the Russian people. It displays public, gallery- quality art at every subway stop and the experience provided me with a greater sense of live interaction with Russian history. It was one of many attractions that I was happy to have seen.

In Moscow I met up with Rudy, one of my 'Emigrobot' Polish friends from London. We decided to try out a Russian steam bath, known as banja. The heat and humidity were so intense that I almost fainted in the pool. Luckily I was conscious enough to get up to take a cold shower before I did pass out.

As part of the ritual of the steam bath, participants are required to buy special slippers to walk in the steam rooms to prevent falling. They are unfashionable fur trimmed offerings that resemble the type of footwear worn my old men in their homes. Despite the teasing I got from my friends about looking like an old man, I kept them with me as a reminder to be careful until a few years later in Cali, Colombia when I finally disposed of them.

Russia, China
"Seven days on a train"

On The Road To Asia

After a few days in Moscow, Rudy and I bought train tickets for the Trans-Manchurian as it was sometimes called from Moscow to Beijing. The route would take us through the northern regions of Russia, past the world's largest fresh water lake, Baikal would eventually turn south and arrive in Beijing seven days later.

A journey of such length can distort time and seem to make the rest of the world disappear. What is left is the train and its passengers cocooned in a separate reality that passes through days and nights that blend together as one seamless experience.

Our train micro-world was filled with both fun and inspiring moments. We met a man named Tony, from Melbourne, Australia who now lives in Rio de Janeiro and with whom I later connected in other places in the world – Japan, Colombia and Brazil. In the circle of global travelers, sometimes the world can seem pretty small.

We shared good times with an impressive international mix of fellow passengers. Rudy and I decided to host a party in our train car. We toured the train inviting people who looked like they would enjoy a get-together and ended up attracting a wild collection of attendees. There were two Irish women in their forties who were teaching English in Shanghai, an Armenian man who always wanted to share his food, a Russian man who apparently was a cocaine addict and a group of young Russian circus artists heading to China to perform. With all the people, loud music, broken English-Russian conversations and free-flowing vodka, foot massages and crazy dancing, it was quite the intense time. The next day, Rudy, Tony and I recovered from our hangovers with quiet conversation.

Our discussions turned to the current popular subject of manifestation and the steps that were given in the book and movie "The Secret":

Does the mantra of 'ask, believe, receive' really work? Can you really manifest what you want by imagining and feeling it? What if everyone could manifest everything that he/she wanted instantly - let's say a red sports car - just by closing their eyes and imagining it? How would that affect anyone's motivation to work towards his/her goals?

We analyzed the case studies from "The Power of Your Subconscious Mind" by Joseph Murphy:

Can you really ask your subconscious mind to solve a problem before going to sleep and wake up with a solution? Shall we act as if something we want is already received?

We talked about all these questions, their implication in our lives if they were true and shared personal experiences. The only conclusion was that, one day we would grasp all the wisdom in the mysterious, new ideas that we were hearing about and contemplating.

AWAKENING INSIGHT
Curiosity and inquiry about the spiritual aspects
of life is the beginning of waking up. There is more
than a scientific aspect to our existence.

The landscape was constantly changing out the window as we made our way from Russia to Asia. Our progress was seen as we exited from our little bubble of reality to buy food at the station stops and noticed that the people were looking increasingly more Asian at each successive station.

We found ways to entertain ourselves as the days passed. In another prophetic moment of destiny that connected me to my future, Tony taught me the Spanish lyrics to a Colombian rock singer Juanes' song "Tengo la camisa negra". Little did I know then that I would stop traveling and live in the singer's native country.

We finally reached Beijing. Rudy and I said good-bye to our friends and disembarked into a weird and completely foreign world. There were signs in Mandarin writing that we could not read and massive crowds of short dark haired people everywhere. We had absolutely no clue how to get to the hostel. Luckily, I had my "Western Asia Rough Guide China" with the hostel address written on the map. We caught the local transportation suggested in the guidebook and after 45 minutes we reached our destination.

Asia

China, Hongkong
"Been here"

Stranger In A Strange Land

From the first day, China was different from anything I had ever experienced before. I felt like a stranger in a strange land. The unfamiliar characters of the written language on the signs had no English translation, which made it impossible to understand any directions.

Before going to China, I had heard a lot about its growing potential as a world power. Although there was a sense of a strong economy, it felt to me like the culture as a whole was repressed. It was hard to reconcile the alleged dominant force in the world status I had heard about with the relatively third world reality I encountered.

Beijing itself was huge and chaotic with evidence of significant poverty. In my interactions with others, I did not find the aliveness of spirit or sense of individualism and free abstract thinking that I had in other countries to date. To me, without this vibrancy and inspired drive, China's potential for greatness as was suggested did not seem possible.

AWAKENING INSIGHT

Philosophers, musicians and artists are leaders who influence and change the course of national history because they add unique value and spiritual inspiration to a country's character.

We soon discovered that the best food in Beijing was available at the small corner restaurants where the locals ate and the menus were only written in Chinese.

One custom we learned and practiced was the art of bargaining, which a British traveler we met eagerly demonstrated to us. He was taking advantage of this form of cheap shopping on his way back to the UK. He had been living in Seoul, South Korea and recommended a famous bohemian bar, OI, in Seoul. It was only known to few people but was supposed to be well worth the visit. As South Korea was next on our journey, we tucked away that information for future use.

Evidence of the significant Communist hold on the country became apparent when I realized that my Google-based blog had been blocked for the "safety" and "well-being" of the Chinese people. The Government censors all media including Google search engines and provides its own social platform that strictly oversees the information available to its people. Communication is power. Whoever controls the media controls the people.

Despite our culture shock and the restrictions, we took time to explore some of Beijing's magnificent sites. The magical Summer Palace and surrounding gardens was a stunning display of Chinese landscapes, open water areas and functional workplaces designed to express the balance between man and nature. The rebuilt Forbidden City was home to twenty-four emperors during the Ming and Qing dynasties and is now a museum and historical site that preserves the beauty of Chinese architecture at that time. It was a powerful reminder to see the remnants of the Chinese glory before Mao Tse-Tung's controversial Communist takeover of China.

While walking in the historic Tiananmen Square, we were approached twice by professional scammers who attempted to con us. Young girls pretending to be impoverished art students tried to sell their cheap art for inflated prices. These supposed art students spoke good English and would target a tourist, often a white male, approach him and invite him to their art gallery for the last day of their exhibition. When there, they would offer a special free gift of a 'personal dream' inscribed on a scroll in calligraphy and then try to sell worthless art for the price of masterpieces. The whole act was set up in such a sophisticated way that the victim would feel very guilty at not supporting these poor artists.

We were inexperienced travellers and not aware of the scam but somehow, thanks to common sense, we managed to avoid the deceit. What caused us to trigger to the con was their almost desperate insistence that not having space in our backpacks was not a problem. They asserted that we could always ship the art home. The pushiness of the attempt to get us to buy alerted us to back away and leave without losing money.

Then there was the tea ceremony rip-off, which was a bit more obscure and more difficult to detect. It started at the same location with two attractive and friendly Chinese students who spoke English. They approached us offering to show us around. Their ultimate goal, however, was to guide us to a traditional tea ceremony, where we would be charged in excess of $100US just for the privilege of sitting and watching the ritual. There would be additional costs if we wanted to participate in tea tasting. It was obvious to us afterward that these young girls were being paid a commission to encourage their victims to try every type of tea available because there was a separate charge for each cup.

When I read the menu, at the bottom in tiny writing, was the information about a cover charge of $100US. When we saw that, we decided to leave and despite the two Chinese guards at the door that caused me some fear, I loudly declared that we could not afford the cover charge and were leaving.

The girls looked surprised that we had caught on to their plan and quickly offered us a place at the free tea ceremony table.

"Ok, but we want to try only two types of tea each, no more!" I agreed cautiously knowing the prices of the tea and that the second free table looked no different than the one we were leaving.

By this time, I did not even care about the ceremony, which was performed rather carelessly anyway. Rudy and I finally left having tasted 8 tiny cups of tea. On the way out, we paid the bill for the originally agreed amount of $16US and certainly left no tip.

I learned lessons from both scams. Since that experience, I am a little less naïve and trusting of strangers who speak good English and who approach me with an offer that sounds too good to be true. I realized how important it was to trust my inner voice even if people in the external world are pushing me to do something contrary to my intuition.

AWAKENING INSIGHT
Always trust your inner voice.
Intuition is more important to listen to than
anyone else trying to convince you to do
something other than what you want to do.

After returning to the hostel, we discovered an announcement posted telling us to be careful of scams by fake artists and people selling overpriced tea ceremonies who were after nothing more than money from unsuspecting travelers. It pays to read the notices in hostels as they are intended to help travelers.

Majestic Ancient Culture

Before departing for our next destination of South Korea, we completed the four-hour trek to The Great Wall. It was massive, wide and snaked along the tops of the mountains as far as the eye could see. The sun shining over the green mountain vistas illuminated the inspiring scene before us. Besides being one of the Seven Wonders of the World, it was also one of the most inspiring ancient architectural structures I had ever seen in my life.

Its construction began in the third century as a protection from barbarian invasions from the north. Throughout history it was expanded and reconstructed to stretch along China's northern border. Predictably there was the typical tourist commerce at the entrance to the Wall. Charlatan shamans were offering prayers while soda vendors were peddling liquids against dehydration.

As I hiked along the top of the Wall on a walkway as wide as a regular street, I couldn't help but be overwhelmed at the massive dimensions of the structure. Every step awakened me to the engineering magic that went into its construction. After the long, tiring walk, our transportation back to the hostel was a cramped vehicle that reminded me I was in China. The seats were rather tiny and there was no legroom even for someone like me who is relatively short by Western standards.

With the visit to the Great Wall mission accomplished, I was ready to move on. China was definitely a country on a growth path with its impressive hybrid economy of ferocious capitalism and passive Communism but I was ready for the experience of South Korea.

South Korea And The OI Bar

South Korea is a progressive country with a healthy, growing economy that has risen from the destruction of the Korean War. Its focus in high tech and heavy manufacturing industries as well as consumer electronics has made it a significant player in the global market.

Our ferry ride from China landed us in Busan, South Korea. While waiting for the bus to Seoul, Rudy and I had some time to tour. Located on the southeast shore of the Korean peninsula this second largest city in Korea is a major shipping center for the country and, with its scenic beaches and natural environment, is a growing tourist destination. We enjoyed wandering through the seafood markets and marveling at the vast array of sea creatures represented there. Before we hopped the bus for Seoul, we even managed some time to hit the beach, grab some rays and take a few pictures.

Seoul, the country's busy capital city, has a population of ten million that ranks it as one of the largest cities in the world. It is a visually surprising metropolis with evidence of its traditional heritage tucked away within its high-rise modern architecture.

The people that we met were welcoming as we toured parts of the city on foot. We watched Tae-Kwando street shows, tasted awesome Korean barbeque and took part in an authentic traditional tea ceremony for free, not at all like our Chinese experience.

On the last day of our stay, we visited the magical OI bar that had been recommended to us by the British traveler we met in Beijing. The bar was not easy to find. It was located on one of the floors of a skyscraper in the affluent entertainment

Gangnam district. The interior décor was well designed and unconventional. With its colorful shapes and forms, it reminded me of the avante garde Gaudi sculptures in Barcelona.

The bar featured a light show that was synchronized to progressive techno music played by a DJ who seemed to be high on drugs. We mingled with local artists and took pictures of some of the Korean women who smiled and posed for us. The drinks were very expensive and the distractions too great for us to fully participate in partying. It was as if we had entered a time machine to the future and had landed in a bizarre, pulsing, abstract mass of modern bohemia. The sensory overwhelm was so great that all we could do was simply look around and observe others. We came away with an awestruck remembrance of our night at the OI.

The next day we ended up in a modern and comfortable bus that took us from Seoul to the seashore once again where we boarded another ferry to Japan.

The Country From Another Planet

Japanese culture is a colorful mixture of exotic, modern and traditional. Everywhere we went during our two-week stay we encountered an eclectic blend of smiling students dressed in colorful fashionable clothes who mingled with skinny young people sporting geeky glasses. Elegant, porcelain faced geishas walking to take care of their secret business flowed seamlessly with the crowds of impeccably dressed office workers and briefcase-carrying executives rushing to their high pressure jobs.

We were so swept up in the extreme friendliness and politeness of the Japanese people that it didn't take long for Rudy and I to be bowing incessantly to each other as part of our natural behavior.

The food everywhere in Japan was delightfully fresh, healthy, diversified and so well presented that just writing about it makes me crave it. In Osaka I paid only $5US for a variety of delicious sushi. In Kyoto I tasted yummy seafood served over rice. Of course, we could never get enough of ramen noodles.

The country is probably the most technologically advanced nation on the planet. Even in 2007, Japanese people were already watching live-stream TV on their mobile phones with clear reception in their underground subway system.

Fukuoka, a modern harbor city on the Japanese island of Kyushu, was our first stop. Its futuristic buildings whose mirrored exteriors reflected the bright sun; its tiny serene Zen gardens and temples that popped up between skyscrapers and offered a peaceful meditative environment for relaxation and its walking paths and shopping areas provided endless invitations to see more. We poked around in some old style computer game shops and took in a fascinating modern robot exhibition.

We were thoroughly entertained the whole time we toured Japan. After Fukuoka, we traveled to the major city of Kyoto, the village of Nara then to Osaka and Tokyo.

Kyoto was a step back in time and into the mystical. Quaint specialty shops, exquisite restaurants built in typical Japanese style overlooking tranquil gardens and abundant Buddhist temples (over 1000 in its midst) spoke to the ancient traditions of old Japanese customs. Kyoto's inspired architecture is reflected in its famed Golden Pavilion so named for its gold-foiled exterior that shimmered its reflection in the pond beside which it was built in 1397. It is one of Japan's proudest landmarks.

At the Jishu Jinja shrine, I met a local woman with whom I had a pleasant conversation.

"Hello! Do you speak English?" I asked her knowing that Japanese are quite shy when spoken to in English.

"Yes, but my English is very bad" She said smiling.

"No, your English is good! My friend and I are looking for this place. Do you know where it is?" I pointed to a spot on the pocket map of Kyoto that Rudy and I had been trying to find.

"Aaah, I do not know, but I can ask somebody!" She asked a Japanese man who was passing by and he showed us the way.

"Thank you! You are very kind. What is your name? Are you from Kyoto?" I asked

"Yes I live here! I need to practice my English!" She replied slowly but happy to have an opportunity to practice English.

"I can teach you if you like? Give me your email and maybe we can go out one day and practice English?" We exchanged email addresses and walked together for a while longer as we chatted.

When I came back to the hostel she sent me an email and I replied asking her for a date and giving the hostel address so we could meet up. The experience turned out to be a rather bizarre event as she showed up at our hostel accompanied by two male friends. If they were to be her protectors, they were not equipped for the job. One of them got completely drunk after just sipping a small glass of Japanese beer. Our date ended rather abruptly when she had to escort her drunken friend back home.

The next leg of the Japan excursion brought us to Osaka.

I loved the modern architecture of Osaka and its powerful presence as a center of commerce. It is home to Universal Studios, an attraction that we readily engaged where we played like children for the whole day. At night, we roamed the city and watched with amazement as it came alive with flashing neon lights, restaurants that served up their signature scrumptious dishes and nightlife that delivered generous helpings of fun.

There is a cultural side to Osaka as well. Thanks to Rudy, who had studied art, I learned about the classic urban architecture of Tadao Ando including his famous Church of Light creation that is a special site in Osaka's otherwise busy city persona.

Osaka was a modern city but the people did not seem stressed. Rather, they were smiling and happy. This fascinating and bizarre culture was colored by my seeing it for the first time. Everything seemed amazing to my eyes.

AWAKENING INSIGHT
Wherever your attention goes, it energizes that reality.
You see what you want to see and are blind to the rest.
"Attention energizes and intention transforms"
~ Deepak Chopra

We took the fifty-minute train trip from Osaka to Nara and spent a day there.

Because of its smaller size, the village of Nara was a refreshing break from the hustle and bustle of the more driven cities in Japan. Nara's main attraction is the Great Buddha statue that is situated in a magnificent temple in Nara-koen. The grounds surrounding the temple offer quiet walks and peaceful moments in nature that allow time for inner reflections.

The time I spent in the temples and shrines caused great curiosity and a deep desire to know more about Buddhism. The smell of incense, the relaxed look on the Buddha statues and the happy faces of the people that were so opposite to the suffering ones I remember at the Catholic churches. It was a completely astounding revelation that this philosophy wanted me to be happy. In the temples and gardens, I had short experiences of inner connection through trying to meditate. Just those fleeting moments showed me what was possible.

We returned to Osaka in order to catch the state-of-the-art bullet train from Osaka to Tokyo.

Tokyo was our last stop in Japan. We spent a night at a capsule hostel where the sleeping accommodations were a tiny cubicle the size of a capsuled cryogenic chamber. The tiny space swirled my imagination into a story that I was being frozen in time and waiting to be awakened at some point in the future. I loved the adventure of this unique experience. On another night, as we roamed a neighborhood near the hostel, we heard great music coming from a house we were passing. We decided to invite ourselves to join in the party and were welcomed enthusiastically by the friendly hosts.

"Rudy, can you hear this music? It is a home party! Let's check this out!" I asked with enthusiasm. We approached a man standing in front of the house who looked like he was part of the celebrations. The doors were open and we heard cool music and crowd noise coming out from the house.

"Hi, is this a home party?" I asked him, feeling him out for his reaction.

"Yes, where are you from?" He seemed welcoming and happy to speak to us.

"We are Polish and we love Japanese culture! We have never been to a proper Japanese home party. Do you mind if we come in?" I asked assuming he would refuse but taking a chance we would be invited.

"Sure, feel at home!" He said and introduced us to his friends. We were surprised and delighted at the invitation. We felt completely welcome and simply joined in the festivities as the party continued with us.

I could not leave Japan without spending at least one night in a classic Japanese hostel. We booked into the small accommodation and spent the night sleeping on a mattress on the floor in traditional Japanese style.

Japan was a crazy place where all our senses were fully awakened to their peak potential. We were never bored and enjoyed an eclectic experience of education and fun.

It is difficult to understand why such a vibrant and peaceful nation puts so much value and focus into working all the time. Do Japanese people really consider it a point of honor to work so hard that they could even die at work?

The Japanese only have eleven paid holidays in a year and are purported to only take half of those off so there is little time made available to enjoy their wonderful culture. It made me wonder just how truly happy they were even though they acted as if they were joyful and loving their lives.

I wished I could have spent more time there to find the answers to these questions but Rudy already had booked a flight back from Hong Kong to London so we needed to make that deadline and we had Thailand yet to visit. After an incredibly stimulating two weeks in Japan, we took a flight to Bangkok. If I did not count the short flight from Vienna to Poland, this was the first flight I took from the start of my adventure in Pisa to Tokyo. All the rest of my travels had been by road or rail.

Thailand
"On the road"

Welcome To Bangkok

Thailand is one of the most popular tourist countries in Asia. It offers pristine beaches, impressive and notorious nightlife, fantastic food and the renowned welcoming smiles of the Thai people.

It is not an exaggeration to say that, with a little bit of creativity and an open mind, many travelers could experience the lifestyle of the main characters from the movie "Hangover II".

At the airport, Rudy and I became acquainted with fellow travelers - a Canadian, Matt and an American, Jason. They breezed through the immigration process but we were not so fortunate. We were rejected because Polish citizens needed a return ticket and $800 Baht (Thai currency) before being granted a visitors visa and we had neither.

I was not aware of the requirement but wished I had checked it out more carefully as we now needed to track down a way to get the cash and purchase the required tickets. After searching for an ATM at the airport, which we could not find, we ended up discovering a store that gave us an advance on our credit cards. We bought our tickets online using the free wifi and our laptops.

We returned to immigration, only to face a half hour wait in line. When it was finally our turn, the immigration officer who did not even bother to look at us, informed us that we also needed copies of our passports. *Again*, we left the line in search of a copy machine and when we returned with the documents, we had to start at the back of the queue, which took more time. After a frustrating three hours, a rude immigration officer finally approved our visas and stamped our passports with, "Access Granted to Thailand".

Our new friends were patiently waiting for us outside and the four of us took a taxi to the famous backpacker street, Khao San Road. When we got out of the taxi, the humidity mixed with the aroma of sweet and spicy Thai food and the smell of gasoline hit us. "Welcome to Bangkok." I thought with a satisfied sigh.

We found the cheapest place on the street to stay. It was pretty shabby lodgings with a broken fan and walls that had not seen paint for ages. I felt like Leonardo Di Caprio in the movie "The Beach". After a short nap, we went out to explore the city.

We tried to avoid the choking exhaust fumes and chaos from the mix of tuk-tuks and taxis taking tourists back from parties to Khao San Road. Instead, we found a nearby restaurant with delicious Thai dishes of stir-fried vegetables and green curry topped with the coconut sauce.

Having satisfied our hunger, we began our sightseeing venture with a visit to the Grand Palace. Built in the late 1700's this magnificent and intricate structure is a signature landmark of Bangkok. It was the home of Thai royalty and government for 150 years and has been described as the 'spiritual heart of the Thai kingdom'. It was simply breathtaking to wander through its complex maize of rooms and buildings. We also scouted out the many Buddhist temples that were everywhere in the city.

At the time I had very little idea about the Buddha and his teachings. I had learned a bit about Buddhism from my friend, Kinga in London, but all I knew for sure was how peaceful I felt when I entered the temples here. I was also aware of a slightly more distant feel in these temples as compared to those of Japan. It raised my curiosity about the same philosophy but its different applications. Without me being aware of it, I was slowly being nudged by the Universe to wake up to a new inner aliveness that I had never taken the time to recognize.

That evening we got tickets for a front row seat at a Thai boxing match. I won a friendly wager with Jason and although it was nothing serious for me either way, I noticed how intensely the local fans reacted to the outcome of the match. It seemed that betting was a significant local pastime.

The competition ended late so we took a picture with the champion and left. We still had plenty of energy for more action so we decided to take in the infamous Ping-Pong show, one of the main sex attractions in Bangkok. On the Khao San Road the many taxi and tuck-tuck drivers were selling the shows. We asked one of them for the price.

"Excuse me, how much is the show?" I asked pointing to the flyer with naked girls that the taxi driver was holding in his hand. "200 Baht each." He answered inviting us to ride in his cab.

"It is too expensive!" I said walking away. I was gearing up to use the negotiating tactics that I had adapted since shopping in Asia. The locals count on inexperienced travelers not knowing that they can bargain about prices.

With some persistence and my best resolve, I was able to talk the taxi driver into a free show with only the cost of the ride to the Red Light district of the city.

We were taken to the other side of Bangkok, passing increasingly dark and foreboding neighborhoods. Eventually, the taxi stopped on one of the narrow streets. We paid him to guide us through such a confusing series of doors, stairs, narrow passages and tunnels that we felt like we were in a drug dealing crime movie. This was indeed a different face of Bangkok.

Finally we reached the club, which was guarded by bouncers dressed in black who frisked us to make sure we had no guns. Through the darkness we could see there was a lighted stage in the middle of the bar. We sat at a table and before we knew it, a server brought us two drinks each and four Thai women for our pleasure. As this was not anything we ordered, we attempted to send the drinks and the women away stating emphatically that we did not order either. We asked for a menu instead.

The server muttered something to us in Thai and eventually brought us a menu and took the drinks away. It was clear she understood English although she wouldn't speak it.

We ordered cheaper beers and tried to get rid of the girls who were begging for our attention. Two of them left and other two stayed. One of them turned out to be a ladyboy, as they called transsexuals in Asia. The other girl was cute but we did not pay too much attention to her as the show started. We came to see the Ping-Pong show and that was all we were interested in.

Soon bikini clad women walked onstage and began their striptease act. Thai people definitely know how to entertain Farangs (the Thai nickname for Western tourists). From the opening act, the show degenerated into progressively more embarrassing and extreme acts.

There was an older woman who came onstage with a birthday cake. She was surrounded by younger women who sang "Happy Birthday" to her while she sat on the stage without underwear, cake between her spread legs and blew out the candles in time to the music. The whole spectacle was rather cheesy and embarrassing to me.

Then the Birthday lady took a string of razors connected together, inserted them into her vagina and slowly pulled them out. We were even further embarrassed and shocked as people applauded.

Just then, three bald guys entered the bar and innocently sat down next to the stage waiting to be entertained. It was clear from the look on their faces that this was their first experience in such a place. They had arrived just in time for the grand finale.

153

The woman started inserting ping-pong balls (thus the name of the show!) into her vagina, opening her legs and shooting the balls out into the audience. She launched them at the bald guys, hitting them squarely on their shiny heads. The spectacle of seeing someone being hit by vagina-propelled ping-pong balls made the show more ridiculous and embarrassing than entertaining. One tourist couple left at that point as they apparently had had enough. We too decided it was just too much and it was time to leave.

We asked for our bill but what they brought was one that charged us an entrance fee, the original 8 drinks and fees from the escort company that the four women were employed by. Despite screaming threats being hurled at us in broken English by the manager, we refused to pay for what we did not order. I stood my ground and insisted that we would only pay for the cheaper beer since the taxi driver had assured us that the show was free. I had to threaten to get the police involved before we had any success and we were free to make our way past the bouncers into the freedom of the night.

Once we left we realized we were only one block away from the infamous Pat Pong Street notorious for strip bars, Farangs and Asian hookers. Seeing as how the night's theme was pretty much the seamy side of Bangkok, we decided to round out the experience. What we saw was more shocking than where we had just been. I have never seen so many prostitutes gathered in one place. Out of curiosity we entered one of the bars and ordered beer. We sat in front of the stage while a parade of about fifty Asian women, all dressed alike carrying a card with their number stood in front of us. They wanted to be hired for the night in order to make money for themselves and an equal amount for the bar owner. They smiled at us, performed seductive dances in front of us and sat in our lap. It was all an act to take our money although we did not think of it that way at the time. We escaped into the street once again as we had no desire to hire a hooker. It was certainly something I would never do.

The night was still young so we decided to look for a more authentic experience. We found a Thai rock bar full of local students. After ordering drinks, we sat down at the bar and listened to live music. I spotted an alternatively dressed good-looking Thai woman who smiled at me.

"Hi how are you?" I asked her.

"Good and how are you? Where are you from?" She was definitely flirting with me.

"I am from Poland, this is my friend Rudy also from Poland and Jason from Canada!" I introduced her to my friends.

"Nice to meet you!" she was sweet and had an upbeat way about her..

"Is this a typical Thai rock bar?" I asked her common questions already knowing the answer just for sake of conversation.

"Yes, do you like rock music?" She asked.

"Yes I do, but I also like all types of music, depending on the situation"

The small talk continued for few minutes and I asked her to dance. On the dance floor, we kissed and were genuinely enjoying each other's company. I suggested that we have sex to which she was agreeable. I told my friends I would be back soon and we proceeded to find a place where we could make out. The hostels were off limits, and the special accommodations of some taxis felt unsafe. We eventually found a quiet, private bathroom down a narrow street in a residential area. The whole experience was crazy and irresponsible but it was also exciting and dangerous to me. When our love-making was over, she immediately held out her hand wanting to be paid

"Okay, 500 Bahts!" she demanded with a business-like tone.

"What? Are you crazy? I thought we liked each other! Besides, I only have 200 Bahts." I was both terrified and ashamed about what was taking place.

She grabbed the money and we left. I was in total shock and felt like a sex tourist. On the way back to the rock bar she took my hand as if we were a couple. I wanted nothing to do with her and asked her to leave me alone. She was very surprised that I reacted the way I did. I discovered later on that this 'pretending to be a couple' was a popular behavior with freelance hookers in Asia. When I rejoined my friends and told them what had happened it was just one too many adventures for the evening. We decided to call it a night and go back to the hostel.

The next day Rudy and I were scheduled to fly to Hong Kong, but even given all the unsavory experiences in Thailand, I knew I wanted to return when I could explore at my own pace. My first impression of this country was of its ambiguous crazy, shameless, wild, exotic culture. It was one big brothel surrounded by magnificent spiritual Buddha temples. To me, there was just more to know about Thailand and I had to come back.

"Not" Gambling In The Gambling Capital Of Asia

Instead of heading directly to Hong Kong, we decided to take a short side trip to Macau because it was an attraction we had heard about and we simply wanted to see. Macau is an Asian version of Las Vegas. This ex-Portuguese colony is known as the capital of gambling in this part of the world.

Instead of losing our money in the casinos however, we chose to walk around the town and enjoy the small local businesses where we could meet the hard working people who were grocers, tailors and craftsmen of all endeavors. It was dusk and they were closing their shops up for the day. We found a local restaurant and ordered up delicious spicy chicken and then made our way to Hong Kong.

Life At The Mirador Mansion

Hong Kong is a steamy brew of tropical humidity, congested traffic, dense population, towering skyscrapers, Cantonese spicy food, and dim sum. It is the home of incredibly skilled martial arts actors Jackie Chan and Bruce Lee and writer/ director Wong Kar Wai's drama, " Chungking Express".

The inspiring, prosperous city of Hong Kong is an ex-British colony still loosely controlled by the Chinese government. It is the third most important financial center after London and New York and is a world hub of trade and commerce. Situated on only 426 square miles of land that supports a population of seven million, it is one of the world's most densely populated areas and the perfect spot for city lovers. The city center is overwhelmed with over 6,500 of its infamous dingy skyscrapers that provide cubicle-like homes to many of its citizens.

My stay at one of the worst and most exciting of these high-rises –the Mirador Mansion– was unforgettable. It was a tiny flat transformed into a backpacking hostel on the 13th floor of an old skyscraper.

Each floor of the building represented a different social class of Hong Kong culture: Arab immigrants selling leather products on one floor were separated from the fake watch traders, Asian hookers, elegant handmade suit designers, low key backpackers, businessman on the contract, law students, and local residents.

There was so much to do on this tiny, overcrowded island.

In the daytime we explored Kowloon, the urban area of Hong Kong where the Mansion was located. We visited Lantau Island to see the Giant Buddha Exhibition Hall at Po

Lin (Precious Lotus) Monastery and took pictures of ourselves in a meditative posture in front of it.

I rode on the top deck of an old British double-decker bus through some of Hong Kong's city center. The Hong Kong addiction to impulsive shopping was evident everywhere. We passed by hoards of young Chinese consumers adorned with a colorful array of bags from brand name stores. Looking at the rush of people on the streets, it appeared as if we were witnessing Christmas madness.

At night, the sky train ride to a scenic overlook where the panorama of Hong Kong's expansive skyline shimmered across the horizon took my breath away. With all due respect to the Manhattan skyline in New York and the Thames River view in London, this was the most stunning city scenic splendor I had seen in my life.

While walking around the streets of Kowloon we decided to check out one of the local clubs. I had a chance to try my hand at dice. As we entered we heard:

"Hi, where are you from?" One of the guys from the table, where they played dice asked.

"We are from Poland, and you?" I inquired with a laugh as it was clear they were locals.

"We are from Hongkong!" They said proudly. "Do you play dice?"

"A little bit but it is better if you explain the rules to us!" I said.

"No problem, it is easy. Come and join us for a game!"

We were introduced to his friends and enjoyed playing dice for a bit while we drank whiskey and sang karaoke with our new local friends. We proceeded to join a street party with them and other backpackers in an unforgettable experience of fun. Rudy and I checked out a local salsa club, where I had my first meeting with native Colombians on the road. I had no idea how to dance but we had great fun anyway.

We headed back to the Mansion in a taxi that took us on a mesmerizing ride through the extensive, modern tunnel that joins the city center of magical Hong Kong to Kowloon. We were filled with the experiences we had shared together but it was almost time for Rudy to leave.

Random Travelers
Affect My Journey

The day before Rudy left for London, we went out to the gringo nightlife spot where we noticed a very special couple in the crowd. The young beautiful couple was hugging each other passionately and they smiled at us as we approached them. We introduced ourselves as I remarked how happy they looked together and asked what their secret was. They told us they had just come from the Philippines where they actually overstayed their visa because they had been having so much fun.

"You have to go there! It is awesome." Both of them insisted with breathless excitement. Up to that point, I had been unsure of my next destination after Rudy's departure. Now, I knew exactly where I would go.

We spent a wonderful few hours chatting with our new friends, Maya from the Czech Republic and Andy from England. Then Rudy and I returned to the Mirador Mansion.

The next day Rudy flew to Poland and I bought a one-way ticket to Manila, the capital of the Philippines. Because Philippine immigration requires a return ticket before granting access, I had to use a bit of Polish ingenuity with the help of my computer to create a return ticket to satisfy their requirements. It worked out well for everyone without creating any problems on either side. Sometimes, the skills learned during my time under Communist rule came in handy.

Filip Ziolkowski

AWAKENING INSIGHT
Awakening has a lot to do with listening, accepting change and letting go of your attachment to the initial plans that were set by your limited mind.

Lessons On The Plane

On the plane from Hong Kong to Manila I met Dan. He was a skinny grey haired, rather short, fiftyish man from the U.S. who lived on one of the Philippine islands. We struck up a conversation and when I told him that I was visiting Manila for the first time, he shared his first experience in Manila with me. It turned out that Dan had arrived in Manila looking only for sex and had ended up on the wrong side of the deal. He told me that he had been robbed in his hotel room by girlfriends he had brought to his room. It happened when he went to use the bathroom.

"I do not know why I am telling you this. I guess I wished someone had told me when I was your age. You are very lucky to know this in advance." He said with a serious voice that sounded like my favorite uncle.

Dan was the first sex tourist I had ever met. I did not quite understand what he was trying to say to me because I was simply a young backpacker looking for fun, adventure and romance on the road. I thought the horror stories he was sharing only happened to old divorced men looking for paid sex like Dan so I never considered I could just as easily become a victim. The conversation did drag me into the world of adults with regard to backpacking. Suddenly, the rules of being a backpacking student no longer applied.

What I did not fully grasp about developing countries was, there were many innocent looking young women who were actually freelance workers in the sex industry. Their targets were the many men of all ages and ethnicities either married or divorced who were seeking paid sex or monetarily based relationship contracts. These unorthodox arrangements either short-lived or long term were quite common here. It was a world completely unknown to me before I came to South East Asia.

It turned out that Dan had not made reservations to stay anywhere in Manila so I arranged for him to join me at the hostel I was booked into. He was familiar with the area so making our way to the accommodations was easy.

That first day in Manila, Dan and I went for a walk at 5 a.m. to find something to eat. We settled into a nearby restaurant where we tried a Filipino delicacy called, Squid Adobo. While we were eating, a white van full of beautiful girls stopped across the street and the young sexy Filipino beauties came into the restaurant and invited themselves to sit at our table. I had to pinch myself to make sure I wasn't dreaming. Here I was a European in Manila for the first time, innocently minding my own business at 5 a.m. in a restaurant when these beautiful women ask to sit at my table.

What I did not know was that they were probably working in one of many nearby karaoke bars, which were really Philippine brothels with music. As much as I thought it was a phenomenal piece of good luck, it really was not quite so significant an event. I was blissfully unaware that the visitors at our table were there more for business than out of spontaneous attraction. I eventually came to understand that in Asia, women were often freelance working girls who really were focused on my money and not on me.

This was proven from a liaison I had with a woman I met on the flight to Manila. We exchanged numbers and eventually met for a date. I was attracted to her and saw her as someone with whom I could potentially have a romantic connection. She, on the other hand, acted way too interested in material possessions and a luxury lifestyle. She viewed an exchange of her sexual favors for my money as a means to achieve her goals.

For me, it was just one lesson in the steep learning curve about the love game, especially the Asian love game.

After a couple of intriguing and happy days and nights in smoky sexy sultry Manila I was tired of the city and decided to head to the northern part of the country to explore.

My mode of transportation was a first for me – a ride in a Jeepney, a jeep-like miniature bus that was colorfully decorated and was the famed method of public transit in the Philippines. The Jeepney made its way up the narrow roads to Banaue, a small town nestled amidst of the emerald green mountains of stunningly beautiful rice terraces. In the municipality of Sagada in Mountain Province, I explored mystical caves and a bizarre display of hanging coffins. The hanging coffins are a traditional type of burial for some of the Philippine people. There are apparently restrictions that suggest only those who have been married and have grandchildren can be buried in this way. I left the area in utter amazement. There was no end to the customs and beliefs that existed in the world.

Diving Meditation With Sam

After my stay in Banaue, I returned to Manila for one last wild night there. The next day, I left for Puerto Galera, a beach area where the diving was affordable and the partying was in abundant supply at night. I decided to learn to dive and found an American instructor named Sam.

Sam was about fifty with long grey hair and a tattooed body. To me, he was a rock star. I loved his stories about how he set up the first diving shop on the island in the seventies and how his future wife had saved him from Philippine jail where he was headed for possessing marijuana.

We dived together a lot. He introduced me to the magic of the underwater world and gave me all the information I needed so that I could fully appreciate the underworld beauty of planet Earth. Finally, I grasped why people spent so much money on diving. It was probably one of the most profound forms of meditation I had ever encountered without really formally trying to meditate. The key, I learned, was to relax, breath slowly, and focus on all that was before you. When I did that, I forgot about my problems and became fully present to each awe-inspiring moment. I realized with gratitude how privileged I was to witness this amazing whole other existence.

AWAKENING INSIGHT

Diving is one of the most profound forms of meditation I had ever encountered. The key is to relax, breath slowly, forget about any problems and be fully present in the moment.

I had heard that Puerto Galera was not only a diving mecca but was also quite a party town. What I did not know was that it was also known to be one of the destinations for sex tourism in Asia. After a week of diving the reefs and partying at the floating bar with extremely friendly locals I had no doubt about the truth of any of these rumors.

In Asia the concept of love and relationship was quite different from what I had grown up with in Poland. Here, many relationships and marriages are based on an antiquated monetary contract between a man who provides luxuries and a woman who provides youth, enthusiastic energy and sex. Surprisingly these kinds of arrangements seem to work.

AWAKENING INSIGHT

Many relationships and marriages in Asia are based on a different value system than in Western cultures. It is advisable to not judge and remain open to the customs and beliefs of others as you travel the world. Not everyone has the same standard or perspective of life and acceptance of that is key to personal growth.

Thanks to Sam, the divers, the locals I befriended and a very affordable cabana with a spectacular view of the sea, I really loved my stay in Puerto Galera but it was time to continue my exotic explorations.

Island Hopping

With my PADI dive certification from Sam in hand I decided to go island hopping. First I visited one of the most beautiful islands of Boracay, where I swam, ate fresh seafood and chilled on the brilliant white sand of Boracay beach. As I warmed my body on the beach, I listened to local musicians play Bob Marley's songs at one of the many beach bars. It was perfect.

I almost ended up on a date with a transvestite who was working behind the bar. Luckily an American woman who was originally from the Philippines saved me because she recognized the difference. She taught me how to tell a woman from a ladyboy.

"You have to tell them to put both arms together. The dead giveaway is that ladyboys will have straight hands and a woman will have a slight curve. It is impossible to correct that with surgery." She informed me. "You should also pay attention to the voice and look at her height. Asian women are usually short."

The last piece of education about ladyboys came from a local I had met in Boracay, " Never approach tall girls when you are drunk."

Personally, I am accepting of others' sexual preferences but found my introduction to ladyboys an eye-opening learning that showed me just how diverse the world really is.

"What crazy but helpful advice." I thought, "I would never have believed when I lived in London that I would have had to learn this on the road."

In Boracay I met Pat, an American man, in a rather unusual way. While I was sitting on the beach and listening to the local band playing the Bob Marley music, a friendly Filippino girl approached me.

"Hi! I saw you on the beach this afternoon. Do you know my friend Pat?" She asked.

"Hi! Nope I don't know Pat?" I was surprised by the conversation that had started so abruptly.

"He is an American!" She said, assuming that I was American too.

"But I am not an American, I am from Poland."

"Poland? Wow, where John Paul II was from? Great! My name is July. Nice to meet you! Do you mind if I introduce you to Pat?"

"Not at all! Nice to meet you July! And nice to meet you Pat!" I greeted both.

Pat was also enjoying the beach music and we started to get acquainted. He was from Louisiana and had survived Katrina. He shared some harrowing tales of that experience as I told him a bit about my life in London. The conversation turned to our travel interests, which seemed to be similar at that time.

We traveled together to the remote Malapascua Island, which was a relatively new dive destination. The journey to get there was arduous and required the use of various transportation systems from local buses to bamboo boats. It took patience and negotiation to get there but in the end it was well worth the effort.

Once we finally arrived, we toured the island and wrapped ourselves in the genuine smiles of the happiest kids in the world. They followed us around with their insatiable curiosity and wanted to know everything about us, who we were and what we were doing.

The next day after a two-hour boat ride to a tiny out-island, I went on a dive to an underwater labyrinth that was nothing short of magic. The area was full of white tip sharks and hidden in the underwater cave was an opening to a small water hole from the middle of the island above. I saw rays of light from the hole above cutting their way through the dark water of the cave and lighting up a huge school of the fish that swam nearby us. I felt like an explorer on a Tony Halik mission.

The next day Pat and I decided to move to Panglao Island and the sparkling white sand of Alona Beach. We took the big traditional ferryboat to Cebu, where together with other Filipinos onboard, I sang karaoke to "Knocking on Heaven's Door", the Guns'n'Roses version.

That night for the second time on my trip, bedbugs bit me. My body was full of red spots, but probably thanks to the resistance I developed from the Latvia episode, the spots were gone in two days.

Pat and I took local transportation from Cebu to Alona Beach and arrived right at the start of the Drag Queen party on the beach. We grabbed some drinks and proceeded to join in the festivities. The next day, we took pictures of ourselves jumping over the Chocolate Hills in Bohol. This tourist attraction is named for the collection of hills that turn brown in the drought season, thus the name. We motor biked like rock stars around the island. It was the first time in my life that I had ridden a motorbike alone. It gave me a giddy sense of freedom and joy that I had never experienced before.

I spent a few wonderful days on Panglao Island and then decided to depart for Indonesia. The Philippines will always stay in my heart thanks to its wonderful islanders, great weather and easy-going beach lifestyle. I felt welcomed and accepted in this culture. I resonated with their positive outlook, spontaneity and present moment existence. It foreshadowed a similar culture where I eventually ended up living – in Latin America's Colombia.

Indonesia and Mysterious Bali

As a country, Indonesia's physical make up is unique and astounding. It consists of an incredible 17,000 islands over 6,000 of which are inhabited by its 274 million citizens. This vast piece of the planet's real estate is also home to more than 400 volcanoes of which an estimated 130 are considered active. The cultural and religious demographic is mostly Muslim with Hindu with some Christian also present which creates an interesting diversity in the Republic that is characteristic of Indonesia.

Bali, Indonesia is one of world's most famous and popular island destinations especially with nearby countries such as Australia and New Zealand. Its topography is a swirling array of hills, mountains, beaches, rice terraces and volcanic lands.

On the first day I arrived in Bali, a friendly Indonesian from Jakarta invited me to share his taxi ride from the airport to the city center. He did not want any money but just wanted to offer spontaneous kindness. His simple act of good will was a big surprise because many of my future relationships with Indonesians were based on the rule: "White is rich, white has money."

AWAKENING INSIGHT
A simple act of kindness can change
people's lives. Do it often.

Kuta Beach stretches along the Indian Ocean side of Bali. It is one of the places where its surf attracts tourists and experts alike to enjoy the challenge of its waves. I decided to continue what I had begun in Australia and started taking surfing lessons there. In the daytime I focused on finally learning how to stand up on the surfboard and do some simple turns while at night I listened to the life stories from the local women that I met in nightclubs.

There were heartbreaking narratives from a single mom trying to survive by selling her services to tourists; a description of a married woman whose only way to pay back family debts was to use sex as a means of monthly income; a tale of life after the collapse of an arranged Muslim marriage and various other accounts of looking for love, security and fun in life. Along with the stories about their struggles, there was always an unshakable belief in the importance of deep family bonds.

I got sick with a cold and flu the first week I was in Bali, which stopped my surfing classes but still allowed me to explore the island. I traveled to the more mountainous, less populated central region of Bali to immerse myself in the culture and artistic nature of the Balinese people. I was interested in seeing the major attractions in the town of Ubud. I wanted to experience the architecture and mystique of the Hindu temples there and to observe young dancers preparing for their traditional sacred spiritual dances and music shows that they dedicated to the gods.

Ubud's lush natural paradise was all around me as I made my way to the famed Sacred Monkey Forest. I walked through the majestic nature reserve and explored the sacred temples within its boundaries. I played with the wild and ferocious macaque monkeys that were everywhere. The expanding monkey population and the high tourist traffic has caused the monkeys to be aggressive sometimes and there are daily stories of visitors being bitten by them. Precautions are highly suggested for personal safety.

On the way from the Monkey Forest to the temple ruins in Ubud, I encountered a pack of snarling stray dogs. They circled around me never taking their eyes off me. Their empty look of rabid hunger felt terrifying. I was alone somewhere in the village and fearful of what they would do. I closed my eyes and started to pray as I inched forward to get away from them. The dogs followed me for a minute or two and then the prayer seemed to have an effect. They suddenly moved back and left me alone to continue on my way.

My earliest experiences in the cathedral in Gdansk had awakened me to the power of prayer and throughout my life it had been a mighty force that I could count on. This experience was no different. I was very grateful to be alive.

From the first moment I arrived in Indonesia, I was aware of a mysterious invisible energy that seemed to follow me. As I roamed the physical grounds of the temple ruins, I was aware of its uncomfortable presence and it did not feel positive. It was surreal, dark and unfriendly as if I had encountered unfamiliar beings from another planet. It was all very bizarre and being on my own left me quite on edge and uneasy.

AWAKENING INSIGHT
Some places have invisible energy that can be felt intuitively. Recognize your own power to identify, work with and protect yourself from any energy whether it is positive, negative or neutral. Prayer is an effective way to work with energy.

As my month's visa was about to expire, I left Bali for the island of Java and new adventures there.

173

Bribing The Police

After touring Bali, I caught the night bus for the ferry ride to the eccentric town of Jogjakarta on the Indonesian island of Java. This island is the political, economic and cultural leader in Indonesia and is home to more than half of the people in the country. Temples and architecture on the island tell the story of Java's rich and ancient history of rule by Hindu-Buddhists in the fourth and seventh centuries; by Islamists in the sixteenth century and its control by the Dutch during its time of colonialism in the eighteenth century. Today its predominantly Javanese citizens enjoy independence, which did not occur until the twentieth century.

On the bus to Jogjakarta I met a local woman who seemed quite friendly. She sat next to me on the bus and started a talk.

"Where are you from?"

"Poland and you?" I asked, already knowing the answer but it made me laugh at how conversations started with such ritual questions.

"Indonesia. Did you like Bali?" She asked.

"Yes and no, depends. I had some good and some so-so experiences, but it is definitely an interesting place to visit."

"Where are you going now?"

"I would like to see the Bromo volcano and then plan to go to Jogyakarta. "

"If you would like to see the real volcano I recommend you come with me and stay with my family in my village"

She seemed very sincere and helpful and told me that her town had the best access to Kelud, one of the many active volcanoes in the Pacific's Ring of Fire chain. She offered me

174

lodging with her family in the tiny village of Blitar. I decided to follow my heart and give it a try. I felt that I could trust her and was happy to just go with the flow anyway, so I accepted her invitation.

From the moment I arrived at her home, I was treated like a king. It felt strange to be so instantly accepted to the point that I was even invited to a traditional wedding in the town. I was unsure how to repay this kindness and when I inquired whether they expected to be paid or not I received an ambiguous 'it was up to me' reply.

The next day her brother and his friends took me to the famous active volcano, Kelud, that had erupted and killed people from nearby villages just a few years before. We had to bribe the police to let us enter the restricted zone around the volcano. After driving through the jungle, we ended up on a road that was partially blocked by the lava. As we drove around the obstruction, I could see where the eruption had scarred and killed the green hills leaving dark brown barren mountains in its wake and burying all living plants under its molten ooze.

The further we drove the more we could feel the burning in our eyes and throats from the sulfur and smoke in the air. We soon spotted the massive rounded shape of the active volcano that was spitting orange lava and spewing stones into the dark brown lake around its central plug. The surrounding landscape was barren and alien. I felt like I had entered into a Star Wars movie.

My companions feared our sightseeing fun could end tragically if we did not move on so they insisted we leave the area immediately. In this region nobody could predict when the volcano might erupt again and there was a healthy respect for its power. I was grateful for being able to get as close as we did so I followed their lead and agreed we should leave.

After spending three days with this family, I paid them the equivalent of $100 US for their hospitality and the next day I was on the bus to yet another famous volcano located further east on Mount Bromo. This 7,600 foot high mountain in the Tengger range of east Java is one of the most popular tourist attractions in the area. It bears the Javanese name for the Hindu creator god, Brahma.

Taking pictures of the sunrise over Mount Bromo is one of the musts of a journey to Java. The best view is accessible on horseback so I rented a horse that took me to the top of the volcano. As the sun peeks up over the smoking chimney from the volcano and illuminates a new day over stunningly barren land, it feels like one has somehow been transported to the planet Mars. I joined a few fellow photographers trying to capture the essence of this almost sacred moment. There was a reverent silence in this experience broken only by the occasional click of a camera as the witnesses tried their best to capture the wonder and awe of the scene before them.

AWAKENING INSIGHT

Nature is always showing us its authentic beauty as well as its power and magnificence, reminding us that not everything depends on us. It is even more apparent while observing the force of an active volcano in the least exotic places.

Indonesia
"Bromo and Kelud"

After my detour to Blitar, I finally arrived at the bustling city of Jogjakarta. It was there I discovered that my video camera and my I-Pod were missing. I determined that my I-Pod had likely been taken by one of the Filipino women I had dated in Manila and the camcorder had most assuredly disappeared during my stay with the family in Blitar.

In trying hard not to show mistrust of the local people who had been so kind, I had intentionally not locked my backpack. However, it seemed to me that a healthy dose of caution needed to be added to the mix of my openness with others. Unfortunately for me, there were more painful lessons ahead to learn on this subject. After these experiences I started to be more careful but still could not discern how to be with or what to expect from locals.

Although the Dalai Lama suggests that all people simply want to be happy, it seems it is possible to perceive completely different ways to achieve that end. My experience so far had shown me a more materialistic approach in the cultures I had encountered in some countries in South East Asia. Sex was given in exchange for material stability and sacrificing one's own sacred body for money was standard fare. Apparently happiness here was equated to monetary and material security.

My last few days in Indonesia were spent in Jogjakarta, a city of 500,000 people that is best known as a center of art and education in the area. Sadly, it has also been the site of deadly earthquakes and volcanic activity that is part of their daily reality.

The touring I did in the area was sometimes very unusual. I had met some locals who had rather unique personalities but were friendly. They were students on holiday and they offered to show me around. Their English was quite good so we enjoyed easy communication.

When I asked what was going on in the city, they had plenty to show me. We attended bizarre concerts and thanks to my new friends we were granted permission to go backstage to take pictures of the local stars.

I visited Borobudur, the site of an ancient Buddhist temple complex near Jogjakarta. Built in the eighth century, Borobudur is the largest Buddhist structure in the world. Its size and architectural complexity were overwhelming to observe. As I was beginning my self-conducted tour, a guide seemed to mysteriously appear out of nowhere and befriend me. We walked around for an hour or so engaged in friendly conversation about the site. She appeared to be a student who was just interested in chatting with a foreigner. I was grateful for the knowledge she offered but it was not long before she asked for money for this unsolicited favor. It seemed that Indonesian spirituality and beauty were able to co-exist with a persistent monetary demand. I had a difficult time reconciling these two polar opposites and was constantly getting caught in their web.

On my final day in Jogjakarta, I dated a beautiful local Muslim woman who, against her family's wishes had recently been divorced from an arranged marriage. I spent an extra day with this brave rebel but soon had to leave before my Indonesian visa expired. As we parted, she shared a saying that she told me had given her the courage to start her life over:

"It is never to late." She uttered as we said good-bye.

I left for Jakarta with her wisdom in my heart.

AWAKENING INSIGHT

It is never too late.

I purchased my train ticket to Jakarta and bought a dozen green mangos at the train station. En route, I ate a couple of the fruit but they were so sour, I gave the rest away. One of the passengers to whom I gave the mangos attempted to sell me items I did not need. In turn, I retaliated with charging him for the mangos. The whole transaction caused the other passengers to burst into laughter, which echoed my amusement at the whole incident. It felt good to share a humorous moment and feel a sense of connection with others again especially through laughter.

Finally I reached overcrowded Jakarta. From the train station it was at least a two-hour trip to the airport and I had only three hours before my flight left. Jakarta had a terrible transportation system yet I somehow had to navigate the chaos and find the quickest way to the airport.

After inquiring, I was advised to take a motorbike taxi. I negotiated a price with my driver and we hit the road. A half hour into a wild drive, the motorbike broke down and had to be taken to a repair station. At the garage, we were offered coffee and friendly conversation as if there was no urgency whatsoever.

I thought I would go out of my mind with worry and anxiety about the lost time. It was all I could do to maintain my composure. Finally, the repairs were completed. We were back on the road, traveling at the speed of light, weaving our way in and out of traffic and expertly avoiding the potholes in the road.

We reached the airport right on time. A few minutes after I boarded the aircraft, the gate was closed. With a sigh or relief, I remembered my friend in Jogjakarta and repeated her mantra.

"It is never too late." I thought with a smile.

AWAKENING INSIGHT

*Never lose faith. Even what seems impossible can
and usually does happen for those who believe.*

No Eye Contact

Singapore is officially a city-state located on the southern tip of the Malaysia peninsula. It is a world-class financial and commerce center with a population of over 5 million. Its citizens seem preoccupied with the normal metropolitan pastimes of shopping, eating, and chasing the latest electronic toys to collect. Interaction with others or engaging strangers with a smile does not appear to be part of their pattern of behavior.

Some say that the eyes are the windows to the soul and maybe that is why it made me sad that I could not make eye contact with anyone on the street in Singapore. It generated that unpleasant familiar impersonal and distant feeling that I had known in London and New York. To me, the simple act of exchanging visual energy shows interest and can make a huge difference in feeling comfortable and connected to each other.

AWAKENING INSIGHT
*The simple act of looking into each other's eyes
without judgment makes one feel like they are
part of the big family on planet Earth.*

Singapore is a city overrun with penalties and fines for even the smallest infractions. Riding a bicycle in a tunnel will incur a fine of (merely) $1000US! The fines and fees were so pervasive I was surprised that there was not a charge for breathing in public. My experience in this city was not unlike the main character in the movie, "The Truman Show", who was trapped inside an artificial reality television show.

In the few days I was in Singapore, I wanted to find something stimulating to do and discovered the impressive, well-designed Asian Civilization Museum. It celebrates the culture and history of Asian evolution and was both interesting and informative. I was happy that I decided to spend some time there.

In tasting the famously spicy Singaporean chicken, my mouth was set on fire from the very first bite. I took a deep breath, drank at least a liter of water and took another deep breath in a futile attempt to cool the inferno.

I know there are travelers who love Singapore and whose experience there has been much more positive than mine. As with everything in life, a preference is partially a matter of being in the right place at the right time to develop perspective.

Every traveler has his/her own favorite and worst places to visit. In my case Singapore was one of the least inspiring countries that did not give me a reason to stay too long. I departed for Malaysia as quickly as I could.

Travel Connections

The country of Malaysia is politically a constitutional elective monarchy and economically enjoys prosperity that is fuelled by its natural resources, commerce, tourism and science. There was not a lot I had intended to see on this leg of my adventure except for the Petronas Twin Towers in Kuala Lumpur and a visit to the National Park, Taman Negara.

The two-towered structure of the Twin Towers is the headquarters for Petronas Group, an oil and gas company of Malaysia and stretches a dizzying 88 stories upward. Completed in March 1996, it took seven years to build.

Tourists can ride an elevator to the Skybridge that joins the two towers or can continue on to the 86th floor to view the panorama of the city below. At night, these skyscrapers sparkle on the Kuala Lumpur skyline and offer a dazzling view from the ground.

My visit to Kuala Lumpur was rather uneventful except for one night as I was heading back on foot to the hostel from touring the city. I had stopped at an intersection waiting for the traffic light when I was startled by a deep voice that came from behind me.

"Hello my friend, where are you from?" I turned to see three basketball player sized women heading toward me in a rather aggressive manner.

It took my breath away and left me considering my escape options. Despite the fact that I asked these ladyboys to leave me alone and told them that I was not interested in their unwanted attention, they continued to harass me. Eventually, the light turned green and I was able to walk away from them.

Further down the street, on the zebra stripes of a crosswalk, I spotted a beautiful woman on a motorbike who smiled and waved at me. In an attempt to leave the ladyboys episode behind, I decided to flirt with her only to find out that she too was a ladyboy. I burst out laughing at the irony of these events and headed straight for the solitude of my hostel.

As I arrived at the hostel, I heard people speaking Polish in the background. It turned out to be a Polish movie that was playing called "Inland Empire". Set in Poland with Polish actors, this movie by filmmaker, David Lynch was one of his most disturbing stories in a string of his many unsettling creations. It was the perfect ending to a night of complete weirdness.

The next day, I was more inclined to experience the natural aspects of the area and embarked on a walking tour of the world's oldest rain forest, Taman Negara. Dating back 130 million years, Taman Negara was established as a national park in the late 1930's. It is home to rare species of animals, birds and fish and is an ecotourism destination that offers canopy walks, cave explorations and bird-watching to its visitors. In the midst of this lush environment, I experienced my first tropical downpour.

When the rain hit, a few Spanish friends whom I had just met and I stopped for shelter at a nearby bar where other travelers were waiting out the storm as well. We all ended up singing Polish, Spanish, English and Malaysian songs and enjoying amiable moments while waiting for the sun to return. One of the people whom I met on the bus to Taman Negara was Pedro, a man from Spain. He and I spent much of the tour talking and enjoyed our time at the bar getting to know each other.

We stayed in touch and I visited him six years later in Madrid where we spent a whole night drinking wine, eating tapas and talking about life and our travels.

Making connections with like-minded people is one of the best parts of traveling. Thanks to the Internet and Facebook it was possible to stay in touch with the many special people I met on the road. In the hostel, I shared the dorm with a super friendly Canadian couple and an American graphic designer from Boulder, Colorado. The American later visited me in Cali on his way to Ecuador. It was one of the aspects I loved about the travel community.

AWAKENING INSIGHT

Making connections and staying in touch with like-minded people is possible thanks to the modern technology. It is one of the best side effects of traveling.

Return To Thailand

Along with other backpackers from England, I crossed the border from Malaysia into Thailand.

This time I wanted to visit the famous Thai beaches and explore the towns. I started with Krabi, which was situated on the Andaman coast of Southern Thailand. Krabi Province is peppered with numerous remote islands framed with magnificent white sand beaches and offers endless bays and coves to investigate. It is said that the area was inhabited an astounding 25,000 to 35,000 years ago. In addition to my usual learning and discoveries, my experiences here were about to teach me some interesting lessons about myself.

Krabi gave me the chance to ride an elephant and take a double kayak tour of the mangroves. While we were in the kayak, my partner a German man in his forties, asked me to take a picture of him. He handed me his small camera and cautioned me not to drop it in the water. I looked at him with some annoyance, refused his inferior offering and flippantly took out my big SLR camera from my bag instead. I totally ignored his concerns and arrogantly decided that his worrying was simply a demonstration of his limited, paranoid thinking.

After the kayaking, I moved on to the island of Phi Phi, which was one of the islands in the Krabi collection. Phi Phi is part of a marine National Park that attracts thousands of tourists to its clear, pristine waters teeming with colorful fish of every description. Its inviting warm white sand beaches are an irresistible part of the experience. While in Phi Phi, I snorkeled with black tip sharks and enjoyed my time with the dazzling marine life. Later at a beach bar, I listened to others' travel stories. While drinking Thai beer, I enjoyed watching Thai musicians perfectly perform American music hits.

The next day I joined an organized tour to Phi Phi's famous Maya Bay where the movie, "The Beach" was filmed. I was like a child tasting ice cream for the first time and did not try to hide my enthusiasm. I took so many pictures of the boat and myself that I got the feeling the other passengers were bothered by my behavior. In my excitement, I did not care about their opinions.

When we reached the beautiful beach of Maya Bay and the movie site, instead of quietly laying on the beach and soaking up the sun, I kept taking pictures. This island truly was paradise. The only reminder of reality was the warning sign about evacuation in case of a tsunami. The sun was so brilliant and warm it made me a bit dizzy but I did not want to miss one minute of this experience by hiding in the shade or losing a photo opportunity.

After two hours we all returned to the boat, which was docked in water a few meters from shore. I waded out with the others but chose to carry my camera strapped over my shoulder rather than put it in its case. As I was climbing the steps to board from the water, a wave came up that shifted the boat. I lost my balance and dropped my camera into the crystal clear turquoise water of Maya Bay. I was standing in shallow water so I grabbed the camera relatively easily. I immediately took the card out and turned the camera on, which was a mistake. I was able to save the pictures on the card but the camera and lens were completely ruined.

I was very upset at this loss and as the boat took off, I realized that the other backpackers onboard had seen what happened yet no one cared enough to comment or offer even mild sympathy. An Australian woman had become cold so I offered her my dry towel, which she took, said thank you but did not say another word to me.

This was pretty typical of the general soulless behavior that I had noticed often in hostels before. In that moment, I felt so lonely, so empty and so very mad at myself for my careless, showy and judgmental behavior of the past few days.

AWAKENING INSIGHT
Life is the best teacher but it takes time to understand
the cause and effect of unconscious actions. Being
careless and judgmental has its consequences.

Now I needed a new camera so the next day I took a bus into Bangkok to go shopping. I wanted the same camera and lens that I had dropped in the sea - Nikon d80 with Sigma 18-200 lens. It took me two days to do the research but I finally found the cheapest seller in Bangkok. I paid half of the price in cash and half with a credit card.

It wasn't until a few weeks later that I realized my credit card was charged an extra 300 GBR for a Thai porn site. It was already too late to identify the fraudulent charges and ask the bank for a refund. All my efforts to find a cheap seller and all the bargaining to buy that camera were totally wiped out with these charges to my card. The whole camera thing was becoming very frustrating and disappointing.

Before heading back to Ko Phi Phi I decided to explore Bangkok's nightlife on my own. I also wanted to check out the infamous Pattaya, a city to the south that was probably the most sexual hot spot in the civilized world. I was curious to see it but after a short time of walking around I was so shocked that I decided to leave.

In comparison to Pattaya, Bangkok was a temple of morality. I had not seen so many hookers' bars per square foot in my life. What was even more upsetting was the number of fat older white men, covered in tattoos, walking hand in hand with thin, young Thai women. It was a creepy reality that I was observing not just a bad Hollywood movie.

Pattaya was a seamy and sexually explicit place that I felt repulsed by yet there I was standing in the middle of it myself. Was I subconsciously attracted to this energy that was both dark and oddly exciting? Bangkok certainly offered this to anyone who wanted to experience it. I could see how one could be drawn into its seduction.

AWAKENING INSIGHT
Traveling in developing countries can be the best teacher of tolerance for the cultures and lives of others.

I wanted no part of the goings on in Pattaya so I returned to Bangkok and took a bus further south to Kho Pha Ngan. I wanted to participate in their famous Full Moon Party. This is the biggest beach party in the world that attracts thousands of young people every month during the full moon.

"Who am I?"

The Full Moon Party Transformation

As the Lonely Planet guidebook for South-East Asia advised, I arrived two weeks before the celebrations in order to procure a room close to the beach. On the boat, I had met two friendly Croatians and together we found a cheap cabana that had two beachside rooms available.

Even though the Full Moon party happens only once a month, there are nightly fire shows performed by local Thai artists as well as musical entertainment at the local beach bars. These activities are designed to attract travelers and increase alcohol sales. This night was no different as my new friends and I made our way to the beach to enjoy the festivities and sample the local drinks.

At one of the bars, I ordered a Thai drink called the "Bucket". It is a concoction consisting of a small bucket of ice, a mini bottle of rum or vodka, a can of Coke or Sprite all topped off with something called Thai Energizer that is twice as strong as Red Bull. I was thirsty and excited about the party so I drank the first Bucket quickly and immediately ordered and drank a second one. As the show started, I was not feeling at all drunk as the Thai Red Bull ingredient hid the effects of alcohol.

The fire show began with one of the performers wetting a long rope with Thai alcohol and setting it on fire. Then an entertainer turned to the crowd and invited a volunteer from the hundreds of onlookers to join in a fiery rope-skipping contest.

It was a game I remembered from childhood that my friends and relatives often played with my grandmother. We would compete with each other to see who could skip rope the longest. I had been quite good at it and often won the competition. However, back then, we wore shoes and jumped on a hard surface. This version was an entirely different experience played in soft sand and barefoot.

Nobody was brave enough to jump first so I decided to show the crowd what a courageous Polish man could do. My ego was soaring with the hidden effects of the alcohol as I stepped forward. The elated feeling did not last long. As I started my jump, I noticed that I was dizzy and sweaty and I suddenly felt the two "Buckets" as they bubbled up in my stomach.

Being barefoot and in sand made it extremely difficult to get the traction to jump. On the first clumsy attempt, the rope quickly snapped back and hurt my foot. I fell down straight on my back. It all happened so fast that I did not grasp what was going on. It reminded me of my first international Judo competition when I was suddenly knocked out by a Russian competitor in the first seconds of the quarterfinals.

With the crowd watching, the Thai performers stopped the rope so I could stand up. I attempted to act cool as I faked a smile and pretended to be fine even though I got up with massive difficulty. I continued to drink more and party with local Thai people and my fellow travelers until sunrise when I finally returned to my room and fell asleep.

The next afternoon when I woke up, I could not get out of bed. I thought my back was broken. The pain was so severe that I instantly panicked and had myself convinced that I would be in a wheelchair for the rest of my life. After a few attempts to get up, I eventually managed to stand despite the intense pain in my back. I decided to try to seek relief by getting a Thai massage but each movement of the woman's hands caused even more pain, especially on my right side. After five minutes of this torture, I stopped the process, paid for the massage and headed straight to a doctor.

"Doctor, I have a terrible pain in my back and I am worried that it is broken." I said, my voice quivering with fear.

"You must have been jumping rope, right?" He peered at me as he lifted his gaze over his glasses.

" Yeah, I did." I admitted sheepishly. I thought of how stupid I had been.

Probably thinking I was smart, he praised my decision to seek his help. "The most important thing is that you came here directly and did not get a Thai massage because doing that would make your recovery longer."

" I did take a Thai massage." I admitted, ashamed of myself and worried what he would say next.

He checked out my back and declared, "It is a muscle. Your back is not that bad. Actually, what happened to you is very typical. I get foreign patients in here everyday. They all come in with the same problem." He continued, "Here is a prescription. When you buy these pills, take them twice a day for twenty days. You should be fine in a few weeks. In the meantime, relax and do not strain your body any further."

I thanked him, bought the pills and slowly made my way back to my room feeling like a ninety year-old man who dreams of nothing but taking a rest. As I could barely move my body, I knew that my lifestyle was going to have to change dramatically.

I rested for few days only getting up to go eat at a nearby restaurant. My back was better but I still felt terrible pain whenever I tried to sit down or make a rapid move. I learned how to walk straight without making hardly any body movement.

It was emotionally painful watching all the young and beautiful people playing Frisbee, surfing and swimming. As I always loved football, the worst was sitting on the sidelines and only being able to observe the beach football competition.

But, instead of getting depressed I decided to use the time to attend to some foot problems I had been noticing. I wanted to get rid of the warts that had been bothering me lately and decided to use a method I had learned from my grandfather's army friend. It involved placing onions in vinegar for a couple of days, chopping them up and applying them to the affected area by securing them with a plaster. Along with this, I added my own daily action of visualizing my feet perfectly healed. Within two weeks, the warts were gone forever. Visualization followed by action worked!

AWAKENING INSIGHT

*Visualization followed by action works even
in the most practical applications.*

One of the Croatians I had met on the boat to the Full Moon Party was named G. He turned out to be a teacher for me. He was a free spirit traveler, windsurfer, spiritual seeker and a big fan of Osho, Carlos Castaneda and Eckhart Tolle. After I had shared my unfortunate experience with my Croatian friends, G recommended two books to read while I recuperated, "The Power of Now" by Tolle and "The Teachings of Don Juan" by Castaneda. Neither of these books was available on the island so each day, G would read me different chapters from his Croatian copies, translating them to English. I began to learn how to apply the principles from "The Power of Now" but Castaneda's "Teachings of Don Juan" proved too difficult to understand at that time.

After a while I came to understand that my back injury was a necessary vehicle for me to experience my first "Aha" moment on the road. Without it, I never would have become aware of the concept of living in the now because that is all that exists. I suddenly understood that I had spent my life living in the past or the future like my culture had taught me. Finally I was learning something completely new about myself and had my eyes opened to a truth I had never considered. At that moment, I did not realize how easy it was to forget about these awakening principles but all in all it was a good beginning.

AWAKENING INSIGHT
Living in the now is an eye-opening concept. How much time in life is spent focused on the past or the future that causes us to miss what is happening in the present moment?

I mostly recovered in time for the crazy Full Moon Party that had been the original purpose of my travels to Kho Pha Ngan. The celebrations lasted all night. At sunrise I was robbed when I hugged an overfriendly ladyboy. Luckily my wallet was empty.

I laughed to myself at this interesting invitation to practice what I was learning, "I am giving away my possessions. I am free of the pain of attachment!"

The party was good but it left me feeling different about all the celebrating than I had before. I saw too many drugged and drunk people and my mind was already into something else, something deeper than attending yet another wild fiesta.

AWAKENING INSIGHT
The first hints of change and waking up begin with noticing that what used to entertain you and give you pleasure somehow doesn't give the same results any more. Suddenly you realize that something else matters more.

The next day I left the island and moved further north to Chiang Mai where I saw an entirely different face of Thailand - the peaceful one. Chiang Mai represents the most spiritual side of Thailand as its hundreds of Buddhist temples and sacred sites give a sense of reverence and heart that can take your breath away. One of its most famous attractions is Wat Suthep, a golden-spired working Buddhist monastery, which was built into the side of Doi Suthep Mountain.

There are places in Chiang Mai where the streets are lined with gongs and prayer wheels. These delightful oases of immense charm and color pop up amid the ugly concrete and pollution of the city itself. Walking through the zen space of a Buddhist garden, a spiritual quote of the Buddha caught my attention and stayed with me in my thoughts: "Selfishness is the real enemy of peace".

That day for the first time, I considered the importance of the concept of selfishness. It felt like the gentlest tap on my shoulder from the Universe...another step in my process of waking up. The seeds of my slowly becoming a different person were being planted and waiting to grow but I did not know it yet.

AWAKENING INSIGHT
The Universe will perfectly guide you from one experience to the next on your path of Awakening. Consider the timing of messages that catch your attention as small and well-placed taps to teach you how to wake up.

"At the center of your being, you have the answer; you know who you are and you know what you want"
~ Lao Tzu

Laos, Cambodia
"Happy Buddhists and Angkor Wat"

Mekong Journey And Happy Buddhists

I crossed the border into Laos leaving the relative chaos and conflicting experiences of Thailand behind. It immediately felt like I had entered a very peaceful country. The low cost of living, untouched nature, friendly people and less tourism than nearby Thailand made Laos a favorite spot for young backpackers.

I began my trip on a slow boat that floated down the dark, winding and mystical Mekong River that was surrounded by wild mountain peaks. The destination of Luang Prabang took us a few days. We were scheduled to arrive the day before New Years Eve. To kill time I played the popular card game of travelers everywhere, "Asshole" and took in the easy going pace of the Laotian lifestyle that I saw in the villages we passed by.

When we arrived at our destination, our relatively large group – there were five of us – had issues finding accommodation in Luang Prabang on New Years Eve. Our group consisted of an Irishman and an Englishman, two Canadian women and myself.

The Irish guy found a room for himself and disappeared without a word. His behavior not only here but also on the boat caused me to judge him harshly as being selfish. He had indicated how much he enjoyed the pleasures of Pattaya in Thailand, which did not endear him to me either. I had a hard time with the way he treated us all and especially one of the Canadian women who had a crush on him. I recalled the

Buddha quote about selfishness being the enemy of peace and could readily see how true it was.

The remaining four of us settled into the one room we could find but I chose to mostly hang out with the Englishman in our group.

That night I attended my first New Years Eve party on the road. I had fun but ended up also feeling guilty about a brief sexual encounter I had with a Thai woman I met at a bar. Despite her pleas for me to stay longer with her after we had sex, I selfishly decided that I wanted to party more and so left her to return to the festivities.

So many times we are so judging of somebody else's behavior that we don't see that very behavior in ourselves. This was a classic example of this truth. I had decided that the Irishman's behavior had been unacceptably self-centered and here I was doing the very same thing. Jesus was quoted as saying, "Judge not, lest ye be judged." It occurred to me that part of awakening might include developing the ability to practice non-judgment.

AWAKENING INSIGHT
Awakening can be recognized by the development
of an ability to practice non-judgment.

On the road it is easy to become trapped in a judgmental
state. Then it is good to remember Jesus' teaching: "First
cast out the beam out of thine own eye; and then shalt thou
see clearly to cast out the mote out of thy brother's eye."

On the first day of the New Year, I learned to match the slow pace of life in Luang Prabang by observing the people. I admired the simplicity of the Buddhist monks dressed in orange clothes who joyfully played football in back of their temple and lived perfectly in the now. It looked like they had nothing yet they had everything simply by appreciating each precious moment of life.

AWAKENING INSIGHT
The secret to happiness and peace seemed to be shown to me
in the example set by the Buddhist monks playing football.
In the joy of the moment, they had everything they
needed. Nothing else mattered and it was perfect.

The next day I arrived at another backpackers' town, Vang Vieng. It is a spot famous for tubing down the Nam Song River. There are stops every few hundred feet that feature bars where one can get a drink or participate in other water-based activities such as rope swings or zip lines over the river. The whole experience was accompanied with drugs, alcohol and loud music so it was not much fun for me after the first two hours. In fact, it was quite depressing to see so many unconscious, drugged young people floating alone down the river.

After I went back home I was feeling very sick. I had not been feeling well for a while and I decided to stop the anti-malaria pills that I had been taking for last two weeks. The next day I was feeling much better and soon had completely recovered. I started to question modern medicine's insistence about following their instructions in order to not negatively affect your health. Their overreacting can sometimes cause more trouble than good.

My last stop was at the mysterious Khmer ruins of Wat Phu in the province of Champasak. These temple ruins date back to the fifth century with the majority of its relics being built from the eleventh to the thirteenth centuries. Wat Phu was only a teaser before visiting Angkor Wat in Cambodia, one of the most spectacular ancient structures on the planet.

Trapped In The Matrix

Cambodia is a country whose history is sadly about extreme violence and social injustice especially during the time of the reign of terror of the Khmer Rouge in the seventies.

Although post-trauma still affects its economy, the resilient Cambodian people do their best to enjoy life and survive - many by working in the growing tourism industry.

On the first day I booked a riverboat excursion so that I could take pictures of the blue river dolphins. I was curious to see these creatures that I learned were actually related to killer whales. Their normal environment is in salt water but they have adapted to survive in certain areas of the Mekong River.

The next morning I took another boat trip from the town of Battambang to Siem Riep on my way to Angkor Wat. I met a new travel mate, Margot, a French lawyer who joined me in some fun along the way.

"Hi there! Where are you going?" I asked a woman whom I noticed sitting alone reading a guidebook.

"I don't know yet, and you?"

"I think I am gonna take the Bamboo Railway. According to the guidebook it supposed to be pretty cool to do! What do you reckon?" I showed her my guidebook.

"Wow, it sounds fantastic, I want to go as well. Sorry. My name is Margot!" She said in a strong but charming French accent.

"Nice to meet you Margot. I am Fil. You must be from France, right?" I asked smiling.

"Yes, but I am not from Paris!" She said with a laugh, as it was something not very welcomed from the French point of view. We started talking and decided to explore together.

The river road we followed was along wetlands where the marsh grasses protruded out of the water. We floated past a bamboo village built right on the river. In spite of extreme poverty, the people looked happy as they waved and smiled at us. We disembarked from the boat at a small town and took the famed Bamboo Railway that used a hand driven old rickety railway platform to transport us along its rails. At the end of an hour, we moved from the Railway and hired a moped driver to explore random villages.

In one town, we passed a Cambodian wedding. We asked the driver to stop so we could watch and ended up being invited to join the celebrations. We enjoyed the abundant food, alcohol and spontaneous dancing. We even presented a symbolic gift to the couple. Margot had to work hard to avoid the flirting advances of a drunken uncle of the family. To ward off any possible trouble, we thanked our hosts for their hospitality and headed towards Angkor Wat.

We stopped in a smaller town overnight where we witnessed a street Thai boxing contest. It was much more entertaining than the one I saw in Bangkok. It reminded me of the choreography in early Bruce Lee movies and was beautiful to watch. The next day Margot went in another direction and I arrived in Siem Riep, which was the nearest town to Angkor Wat.

There are only a few ancient structures that can compete with Angkor Wat in terms of magnificence, mystery and attention to details: The Great Wall of China, the Pyramids of Egypt, the Mayan Pyramids in Mexico and Guatemala, and Machu Picchu in Peru. Built by the Khmer King Suryavarman II in the twelfth century, it is the largest religious structure in the world.

I bought tickets for three days and explored all the ruins on my own. The complex is situated deep in the Cambodian jungle in the 400 square kilometer area known as Angkor Archeological Park. The area was so expansive that even the large number of tourists at the site did not affect the magic of the place.

As I studied the intricately carved ancient sculptures covered in the spider webs, I felt the mystery around every corner. Just being in this incredibly historic and spiritual energy set my imagination flying about the days of the Khmer Empire and what it must have been like to actually live in these once lavish surroundings. What type of rituals did they perform here? The beautiful typography of the Khmer language added more intrigue to the experience. The time spent exploring all that I did was worth every penny I paid.

After the intensity of exploring Angkor Wat, I wanted to unwind so I went to the nearest nightclub, where I met a beautiful Cambodian girl who appeared to be a student. I got to know her and asked her if she wanted to come to my place. She agreed. As we were leaving the club for the hostel, I was informed at the door that I had to pay if I wanted to leave with her. It came as a shock that left me feeling like I was trapped in a matrix.

I didn't know if I was just choosing wrong places or if it was simple bad luck but it seemed that anywhere I went I bumped into prostitutes asking for money. How had I been deceived again? Had I not learned my lesson yet? What was wrong with me or even worse, what was so fucked up about the world that there were 'pay for sex' situations everywhere?

I left the bar alone, totally confused and disappointed. The charm of travel romance had vanished.

On the way to my hostel some attractive looking hookers who obviously worked for the local brothel called out to me. I was not emotionally interested but my sexual energy was up and guiding my decisions. After a short conversation with these women, I decided to pay for sex for the first time in my life. I had never been to a brothel but figured I had nothing to lose - no girlfriend, no obligation and no potential for finding true love.

"It really is no different than so many of the women I have been with in this part of the world who appeared to be seeking more that just a love connection." I thought, justifying my actions to myself. If I had been completely honest I would have admitted that I just wanted to have sex.

Negotiating the price and picking the woman was very uncomfortable. The cheesy décor of the room and the less than attractive look of the woman totally turned me off from my original desire. The moaning and noises coming from other rooms seemed to wake me to the truth that I was in fact in a brothel, which made me want to leave the horrible place right away. After a few minutes of a rather stressful massage that was all I could endure from the woman, I gave her $20US and left the place as fast as I could, promising myself to never to repeat this experience.

AWAKENING INSIGHT
It sometimes takes repetition to finally learn from past bad choices. Asking the important questions and realizing you have options beyond being trapped in old patterns is the path to change.

After Siem Reap and Angkor Wat, I traveled to Cambodia's capital city, Phnom Penh. Beautifully situated at the convergence of three rivers including the Mekong, Phnom Penh has grown rapidly in recent years and is the political and economic center of Cambodia. Against the backdrop of its progressive activities, I explored the shocking war memorial containing thousands of skulls from the country's violent history in the time of Pol Pot and the Khmer Rouge. It left me feeling great compassion for the suffering of the Cambodian people and in admiration of their ability to carry on with their lives. It was a great example to me of how persistence and resilience can overcome any hardship.

It took me thirty-two years to have my first warm, sunny and snow-less birthday party on the beach. I was born at the end of January in Poland. It was always the worst time to organize a birthday celebration because of winter exams and because it was the coldest and darkest month of the year. This was not the case in Cambodia where the weather was great, the sky was clear and the sun shone warmly on the beach in Sikanoville where I decided to go for my birthday.

Although my close friends were far away, I celebrated this day in style. I ordered wine and delicious seafood and shared it with cordial people I met. Refreshed and happy, I was ready for Vietnam.

History Class From
Another Perspective

My first experience of Viet Nam was the exquisitely beautiful Halong Bay. Natural limestone structures rise out of the emerald waters creating captivating views from the boat of inlets and caves that we eventually explored. Onboard the boat, I passed a pleasant time with an eclectic group of cordial travelers from France, US, Ecuador and Australia. Although the weather was rather cold and misty, it added a special dimension to the whole experience. The surrounding mountains seemed like they were hiding many myths and stories of the people who lived there.

Saigon was my next stop. It was impossible not to be immersed in the chaos of the city with its thousands of crazy moped drivers that made crossing the street safely an art.

I was very interested in visiting the war memorial to find out about the history of the Viet Nam war aside from the fictional versions in the Rambo movies I had watched.

For me, it was easy to understand the effects of invasion by another country because I lived through similar circumstances and history in Poland. When I think about modern day conflicts such as Iraq, Afghanistan, Vietnam and Syria I have to ask myself who or what kind of ideology is behind these senseless conflicts and aggressions? It does not seem fair that superpowers such as the U.S. insert themselves into the affairs of other countries. The Iraq war is a perfect example of this kind of wrongdoing. My personal history as a Polish citizen gave me a certain empathy for the horrifying effects of war and take overs by foreign powers.

From the time of the Second World War, Poland had been attacked, invaded, millions of its citizens exterminated by Hitler and its ancient structures destroyed. It had been betrayed by its allies and pawned in peace settlements that delivered it into the hands of a psychopath, Stalin. His rule eventually led to the brutal communist rule by Russia and economic collapse in my country.

In nature, one animal kills the other only to survive, defend itself or protect its babies. It never attacks on a massive scale to kill for the fun of it or because of its lust for power. So what is the point of one country attacking another ...for the economic benefits, territory or natural resources? How many innocent people have died in order to benefit a few political, military and commercial businesses that make money from war?

AWAKENING INSIGHT
In nature, one animal kills another in order to survive, defend itself or protect its babies. Violence simply for the sake of violence or as an act of aggression will only attract more violence and aggression. The answers to conflict lie not in war but in mutual regard and respect for each other.

The Viet Nam War had actually been a civil war between Communist forces in the North against non-Communist government of South Viet Nam. United States had entered as an ally of South Viet Nam against Communist backed North Viet Nam. The outcomes were not good for the U.S. and resulted in their eventual defeat and the fall of South Viet Nam. This gave rise to the present Communist state of Viet Nam today.

Some Hollywood super production movies such as "Apocalypse Now" and "Platoon" told the complex story of Viet Nam and its horrific effects on people. Other Hollywood movies such as Rambo are pure fantasy and tend to falsely glorify the American might in Viet Nam.

AWAKENING INSIGHT

Hollywood production fiction stories should be treated as such. Often movies either glorify a historic moment or they study a small segment of history in a very personal way. In either case, they are not to be considered as fact.

In Saigon today, the present Vietnamese government rightfully sees the war as won by them. They perceive the American soldiers of the Viet Nam War as clumsy and violent men who killed thousands of innocent civilians, including children, elderly and women in a useless attempt to prevent Communist North Viet Nam's takeover of non-communist South Viet Nam.

The question of who won the war reminded me of my history lessons in school in Poland. We were taught false history lessons that only ended up convincing me not to believe authority. I remember when I was fourteen-year old student and the old socialist political system collapsed. Our history books had to be replaced with new content, stating that the Russians no longer were our allies. My experience of history was that it was a very fluid story that changed as easily as the direction of the wind.

Ultimately, it really didn't matter who won or who lost the Viet Nam conflict. In the midst of exploring this war-torn country, I wondered how many more lives had to be senselessly taken for mankind to understand that violence only provokes more violence and war is not a solution.

I booked the tour to the Ho Chi Minh tunnels with a local travel agency. These famous tunnels were a complex and extensive underground system used by the Viet Cong against the South Vietnamese and Americans during the Viet Nam War. During the guided tour I saw the clever booby traps devised by the Viet Cong and actually walked in the Ho-Chi-Minh tunnels. Trying to breath the limited air underground and being in those cramped spaces offered a stark, less heroic reality that had nothing to do with the portrayals in the Rambo movies.

My guide was half Vietnamese and half American and had served in the American Army during the war. After the war ended, he did not enjoy living in the U.S. and decided to come back to Vietnam. The present Vietnamese government hated him for his perceived betrayal. He also felt he had in some way fought against his own people although at the time the American army was in support of South Viet Nam. The Vietnamese government hired him to work as a war guide so he could show tourists both faces of the war.

AWAKENING INSIGHT
The best way to understand historical conflicts is to travel, listen to both sides and don't take anyone's word for granted. The truth about war is complex and never easily known.

After my history lessons, I had the privilege of spending time with a local family that changed my perception of Vietnamese people. I found them to be intelligent, proud and hard-working people with a great sense of humor.

As I had had enough of war topics, I decided to learn some new skills at Mui Ne Beach a few hours east of Ho Chi Minh. I rented a moped to ride in the city and took few classes of kitesurfing. Riding the moped was easy but kitesurfing was a whole other story that required both muscles and practice. I enjoyed a few kitesurfing lessons and was able to surf out and back to shore successfully but it made little sense to go further as it was expensive and I was soon to leave for India.

On the beach I met friendly backpackers from around the world. There was a couple from Holland, two British students, a neurotic Jewish girl from New York whom I met in Brooklyn six months later, a Dutch girl who had recently been robbed on the bus and an American guy who turned out to be the ex-owner of a hostel in Costa Rica. We enjoyed playing different social games together and passed a pleasant evening getting to know each other.

After Mui Ne Beach, I wandered around the charming, magical ex-French colonial town of Hoi An, biked around Hue and explored the misty grey Vietnamese temples. I walked around backstreets of Hanoi and tasted delicious bowls of local soup. It was an uncharacteristically quiet and peaceful exploration.

On my last day in South East Asia, I celebrated Valentine's Day with a cute Swedish traveler. We ran into each other twice in very random yet synchronous situations so it looked like it was meant to happen. It was also my first date with a white girl since Russia. We had a fun time together and just before I departed for India, we exchanged emails but never did see each other after our brief time together.

I had so many questions about what I had begun to sense about life and love from my travels so far. I was looking for answers and I hoped to find them in India.

India
"Laughing man"

India - Love It Or Hate It

After my experiences in Southeast Asia, India was a completely new world. My planned three months there was less focused on the pastimes of partying and dating locals and more oriented towards learning about myself, seeing more of the world and finding some answers to the questions that had begun to surface – questions about the meaning of life, my personal power and how that knowledge could help me achieve my life goals.

Formerly a British colony, India gained independence in 1947 due to the non-violent efforts of its famous activist leader, Mohandas Gandhi. Today, its over one billion citizens enjoy democratic republic status in an ethnically and religiously diverse culture. Since the 1990's, India has been regarded as one of the world's fastest growing economics and has always had a global reputation for spirituality.

From the moment of my flight's arrival in Chennai, the country offered a complete assault on the senses. I could not help but notice the bursts of color everywhere –in the carved painted temples, in the streets filled with women wearing brightly hued saris and at the almost continual civic celebrations and spiritual festivals filled with smiling, excited people. The hot, humid and sunny days were filled with the noise of everyday life activities where the sing-song dialect of Hindi mixed with other languages in the crowded streets. I loved the energy of the busy markets filled with vendors selling their products, the proximity of the sea with beaches nearby and the rich green of palm trees and rice fields in the surrounding countryside. I was in awe of the huge stone carvings and intricately etched images in the sacred temples, which told stories of the wisdom and the history of this ancient nation.

In India, religious ceremonies and weddings are part of daily activities. They literally happen on every corner in most of the cities and are easily found due to the parade of colorfully dressed people, the smell of exotic sweet perfumes, the sound of melodic prayers and the cows and elephants that were also part of the celebration. The backdrop of these festivities included monkeys that were everywhere, dogs loping their way along the streets, bats swooping down occasionally and birds singing. An invisible energy in the air made me stop and stare in amazement at this entire crazy dance of the universe.

Lesson On The Bus

From Chennai, I boarded a bus for Mamallapuram, located on the southeast coast. This city was my first introduction to India. It was an ancient seaport whose origins dated back to the first century when it was the jumping off point for traders headed to Southeast Asia.

On my first day in Mamallapuram, I enjoyed a conversation with a stranger on the local bus that surprisingly led to discussions about energetic points in the body called chakras. I learned from him that every human being has seven principal energy points responsible for their health and the flow of energy on the physical, emotional, mental and spiritual levels.

AWAKENING INSIGHT
We are more than just physical. Part of being alive includes energetic points in our bodies called chakras that are linked to health on all levels of our existence including the spiritual.

I wanted to know more about chakras and did some further reading and studying about them. It gave me an amazing insight into the function of my body and how important energy is to my well-being:

The Chakras

The first chakra is called Mulandhara or Root Chakra and is located at the perineum, an organ between the anus and the sex organs. This chakra is responsible for the functioning of the adrenal glands. It is related to security, stability, survival and connection with the Earth. It holds the frequency of the color red and is associated with the sound "Lam".

The second chakra, Swadhisthana or Sacral Chakra has the frequency of the color orange and the sound "Vam". It is located just below the belly button in the area of the sacrum. It is responsible for the functioning of the gonads and the production of sex hormones and reproduction. It is related to basic emotions, pleasure, sexuality, creativity, joy and spontaneity.

The third chakra called Manipura or Solar Plexus holds the frequency of the color yellow. It is related to metabolic and digestive systems that convert food into energy. It is responsible for our personal power and sense of individuality. The mantra sound is "Ram".

The fourth chakra is called Anahata or Heart Chakra and has the frequency of the color pink or green. It is located in the chest where our physical heart resides and is said to be the most powerful of the energy centers. It is responsible for the functioning of the heart. It is also connected to our capacity to love, to be compassionate, to experience unity, peace and well -being. It also regulates the immune system. It can be activated by the sound "Yam".

The fifth chakra is called Vishuddha or the Throat Chakra and has the frequency of the color blue. It is responsible for the communication and expression of our will and our desires. It is associated with the mouth, thyroid and neck. It can be activated by the sound "Ham".

The sixth chakra vibrates at the frequency of the color violet and is called Ajna or Third Eye Chakra. It is linked to the pineal gland and regulates clear intuition, insight and visual consciousness as well as sleep processes. It can be activated by the sound "Om".

The seventh chakra vibrates at the frequency of the color white and is called Sahasrara or Crown Chakra. It is our direct connection with the Universe and is the seat of pure consciousness. It is located at the crown of the head and is responsible for inner wisdom. People who activate this chakra are able to live from the source.

~

It seemed as if my inner desire to know more was delivering the information I needed. The next day I met a Japanese woman who, like me, was a seeker. She was reading a book entitled, "The Monk Who Sold His Ferrari" by Robin Sharma, which she recommended. I bought it and, although initially it did not ring my bell, a few years later I re-read it and found a lot of wisdom in its powerful and inspiring content.

We explored Mamallapuram together viewing sculptures and visiting many ancient temples that included the Shore Temple. It was a magnificent structure built right at the seashore in such a way that it allowed an inflow of seawater to transform certain areas of its interior into a water shrine to the gods Shiva and Vishnu.

The sights of the city were a patchwork of its life. There were happy mothers carrying their children, a man on a bicycle in madras plaid clothing that looked like pajamas and free roaming cows that are considered sacred in India.

I marveled at the artisans who still carried on the ancient traditions of telling stories by sculpting large monuments out of huge boulders of stone. I strolled the beach on my own and came upon a young artist vendor sleeping with his child. I watched as women in their brightly colored saris enjoyed bathing in the sea.

Men posed for my camera in front of their boats. I heard an amazing story about a massive stone that had saved a local man from a tsunami. In a sanctuary for dangerous crocodiles, I learned about the process of producing medicine from snake venom. Everywhere I went free-roaming monkeys appeared along my path.

The street vendor stalls were filled with intriguing delights. I was thoroughly amazed at a young man's performance of an impossible trick in which he easily bent his thumb backwards until it touched the top of his wrist.

That night, the area came alive with music as everyone pitched tents on the shore and relished food and community at one of many local celebrations.

"Heaven can wait...avoid speeding"
~ sign in Mamallapuram on a busy street

The highlight of my stay in Mamallapuram was visiting an orphanage and school to have fun with the children. They did acrobatic tricks, played games and posed for pictures with me. Their genuine simple joy and innocence inspired the child part of me again. It was good to feel like I had in the Philippines and Laos.

India promised to be a totally new experience and my first introduction in Mamallapuram only increased my curiosity and desire to know more, see more and open to all that was available to be discovered on my road to awakening. The next adventure awaited in Pondicherry.

"Who am I?"

"What do I want?"

Happy Faces, Positive Energy

As I walked along the streets of Pondicherry, the French influence in its buildings were crazily blended with the Indian culture as colorfully painted elephants plodded their way past the colonial architecture.

One of South India's most popular tourist destinations, it boasts four very popular beaches with names that reflect the interesting mix of metropolitan and spiritual influences in its history – Promenade Beach, Paradise Beach, Auroville Beach and Serenity Beach.

Pondicherry is home to an experimental ashram created by Indian guru, Sri Aurobindo that is named Auroville, which means City of Dawn. It is meant to be a sanctuary for men and women of all nationalities and beliefs to live together in peace and harmony. I did not actually visit the ashram but wondered if perhaps the energy from this establishment spilled over into the town because of its peaceful feel.

The short connection with Pondicherry ended as I headed to more visual delights of Madurai.

The city of Madurai is said to hold the soul of the Tamil Nadu State where it is situated. It claims the status of being one of the oldest cities of India whose history includes trade with the Roman Empire.

The many temples of Madurai include some of the most magnificent that I have seen. Meenakshi Amman Temple, one of the greatest temples in India simply took my breath away with its dark mystery and intriguing mythology. After a short visit I felt a sense of high vibration and meditative reverence that stayed with me for the day.

I spent my time in Madurai absorbing the positive energy from meeting happy people, friendly couples and engaging the pure innocent joy of the local children.

The next day, I reached the quiet town of Kanyakumari, with a sense of well-being and high energy from my experiences in Madurai

Kanyakumari was simply a quiet, warm and amiable respite where I had the pleasure of watching Indian families swim in the ocean. It was a place where pilgrims trek to the Temple of the Virgin Sea Goddess and honor the location of the town at the southernmost tip of India's mainland.

From there, I headed northward up the west coast of India towards Kerala. There were many fascinating traditional festivals, tasty Indian foods, and new adventures waiting for me within the borders of this amazing country of contrasts and spirituality.

Southwest India, Varkala, Hampi, Alappuzha, Kochi

Varkala is an ocean shore town in the state of Kerala whose unique rugged, cliff-lined coast is unique to the area. The water from the fountains and streams that pour from the sides of these cliffs are considered by the locals to be holy.

Bodysurfing on the Indian Ocean waves, yoga classes and my first taste of delicious Indian food of fresh tuna and shark cooked in a creamy, sweet Indian curry sauce made for a pleasant and fun time in Varkala.

On the train to Hampi, my next stop north, I had the opportunity to sample more Indian food – this time it was finger food that I thoroughly enjoyed as I spent time chatting with a local family while we made our way to our destination.

The small village of Hampi had a laid-back atmosphere that made me want to stay and relax into the slow pace of life. Hampi's spectacular sandy landscapes strewn with debris were the result of years of volcanic activity in the area.

At the center of the Hampi Bazaar is the Virupaksha Temple. It is the city's oldest monument that was built in the thirteenth century and was dedicated to the god Virupaksha, considered to be a form of the god Shiva. The temple enjoyed a constant traffic of monkeys and cows passing through its impressive structure that towered almost 150 feet above the town.

One afternoon as I sat at the corner of the Hampi Bazaar watching the people coming out of the enchanting Virupaksha temple, I heard increasingly loud screams coming from the street vendors and shoppers in the market area. In the cascading chaos that I was noticing, there was the sound of hooves on pavement accompanied by a cloud of dust that got thicker with the passing seconds. Suddenly, out of the fog of dirt and upheaval, emerged a panicked looking cow with a massive bull in hot pursuit of her.

Apparently the bull was completely focused on having sex with this uncooperative partner and nothing would stop him from being successful on his mission. The narrow streets lined with vendor stalls were no obstacles to his desire. In a flurry of goods flying in all directions, the bull totally demolished everything in his path.

After the passionate scene passed by me, all I could see was a dense cloud of colorful spice powder in the air. I heard the path of the running animals in the eruption of screaming people far away. Obviously, the bull was not about to give up.

I was so frozen by the drama that I forgot to take the camera out of my bag. As I was catching my breath, the vendors calmly put their stalls back together and set up their pyramids of curcumin powders on the carpets again. Within ten minutes, it looked like nothing had happened. For me, however, it took some time to try to grasp what had gone on and to get my head around how quickly all was restored...just one of the many surprises that would be revealed to me soon.

"Such is the nature of the people of India." I thought.

That day, I shared a tuk-tuk ride with a fellow traveler, a woman from Israel. After our short ride together she agreed to join me on a romantic moped ride to the beaches.

We swam together and then visited a nearby village that was off the tourist path. It was obvious that the villagers had rarely seen a white person. My companion was very uncomfortable in this situation but I loved every minute of making new friends in these unusual circumstances.

After some memorable times in Hampi, I was enroute to another distinctive town, Alappuzha. This village offered a unique break from the usual menu of attractions in India. I passed a pleasant afternoon on a houseboat tour of the backwaters and canals of this oldest planned town in the region. The excursion delivered amazing views of the waters and the people living along the shores.

Alappuzha's major industry is the production of a substance called coir. Coir is the fibrous part of the coconut that is harvested and used for stuffing in cushions, making ropes and weaving mats as well as manufacturing fishing lines.

I stayed briefly in Alappuzha and eagerly looked forward to the next town, Fort Chochin and whatever was next.

Fort Chochin or Kochi as it is also known, was another short stopover where I was astounded at the multi-cultural influences that this historic town demonstrated. Chinese fishnets, Portugese colonial architecture, Hindu traditions, Jewish synagogues, Dutch presence and British influence live together under the tropical climate of the historic town of Fort Cochin.

I moved on to Karnataka State.

Karnataka State is home to Mysore's Maharaja Palace, the Bali style temples of Belur and the Kama Sutra temples of Halebid. Historically, Karnataka was home to philosophers and musicians and those literary influences still survive today.

Maharaja Palace

The greatest attraction in Mysore is the Maharaja Palace. Next to the Taj Mahal, this Palace is the most popular tourist attraction in India. Its impressive entrance presides majestically over the royal structure that was originally constructed in the late 1300's and re-built in 1912. One of the most stunning spectacles I witnessed was the magnificent profile of this Palace illuminated at night. It is an inspiring vision that uses over 100,000 lights to create the art against the night sky.

During the day, I thoroughly enjoyed exploring Mysore's Deveraja fruit market where the scents from the herbs, spices and abundant flowers were exhilarating. I admired the perfectly arranged goods that were sold from very precisely designed vendor stalls. Spending time with the locals in this beautiful setting was memorable.

The next town on my route was Halebid, on the southwest coast of the Karnataka state. The walls of the temples in Halebid are an endless ornate depiction of animals and human figures that tell the story of the medieval culture of India. One of the most powerful series of etchings is the Kama Sutra art that expresses explicit sexual activities and is everywhere in Halebid temples. In the Hindu culture, sexuality is seen as an expression of Divine force and as such, temples honoring sex were a normal perspective of living a life dedicated to the gods.

Similarly, the temples in Belur, a sister city to Halebid share this same culture. Like Bali's style, the fronts of the temples are adorned with intricate engravings of animals of significance to India - elephants, lions, horses – as well as characters portraying Indian history and mythology as well as sensuous and erotic images.

Gokarna was a pilgrimage destination for Indians and is fast becoming a tourist attraction because of its exquisitely unspoiled beaches. The most famous was called Om Beach, so named for its shape similar to the sacred symbol Om.

At the time I was in Gokarna, the Shivaratri Festival was in full swing. It was a nine-day celebration that ended with attendees carrying a statue of Lord Shiva or Mahabhaleshwara as he is also known, in a procession through the main street of Gokarna. The idol is carried on a large vehicle called Dodda Ratha that is pulled with thick ropes by more than 100 devotees. Priests chant and sing hymns in praise of Shiva. Part of this ceremony includes people throwing bananas into a wooden cart as an offering to Lord Shiva. Gokarna's population swells during this time as more than 20,000 pilgrims come to attend this honoring of Shiva.

Although Goa is India's smallest and one of its least populated states, it enjoys the status of being the country's richest area and a center of tourism for international and national visitors. The few memorable weeks I spent in Goa were the real deal. Its beautiful beaches on the shores of the Arabian Sea, rich biodiversity, intriguing mix of religions and architecture as well as its healthy infrastructure provided an enviable quality of life.

After having spent the last few months in morally questionable circumstances in Southeast Asia, I decided it would be a good idea to get tested for HIV and was very relieved to find out that I was clean. I was freed from that worry and ready to explore the mysteries of life in India.

The village of Palolem was the first stop in the State of Goa. Palolem is a paradise for tourists from Europe. It has gorgeous white sand beaches, a relaxed environment and great weather year round. Its Portuguese influences, along with amenities like beer and electronic conveniences, created familiar surroundings for its European visitors. The costs are very reasonable and it is a relatively close distance from Europe by plane.

Music, Shaved Head And New Freedom

When I arrived, my first destination was the beach where I stayed in a beautiful ocean-side cottage with a spectacular view of the sea. I played football in the sand with a group of men and was witness to one of the most dramatic thunder and lightning storms I had ever encountered.

It had been a while since I had thought about music but suddenly I had the urge to learn some new songs in English and practice. I bought a guitar from a local shop and joined a band at one of the beach parties where many people were getting high on drugs. No matter the circumstances, I loved reconnecting with music even if it was in such a basic way.

The weather was becoming increasingly hot and in a moment of sheer boldness, I decided to cut my hair off completely. My new shaved head look was so freeing. It felt like I had cut away all the heavy energy of parts of my journey and had adopted a whole new identity.

As I traveled by bus from Palolem to Anjuna, the window at my seat had been decorated with stickers of Ganesha and Jesus Christ. I was struck by the tolerance that this represented and how it was my experience so far in India. Each day I found reasons to open to this Eastern culture. Here I felt less judgment from others and noticed more acceptance. It was even becoming easier for me to see Jesus as a spiritual being who was not in conflict at all with the Indian gods and deities that I had recently discovered.

Celebrating The Holi Festival

I arrived in Anjuna in time to celebrate the Holi Festival. An ancient Hindu rite of spring, the Holi Festival is a celebration that begins with a bonfire the night before the revelry. The next day, participants shower colored powders over everyone in a wild frenzy of partying and drinking. No one is exempt from participating. If you are in the streets, you are part of the event.

I rented a cheap moped and dressed only in shorts and shades, bought the required plastic bags full of colorful powders and drove around town and to the beach looking for a party. I didn't have to look very far!

Everywhere I went, I saw the smiles of the Indian people acting like kids, laughing spontaneously and having fun in the natural way Indians seem to be able to do. Sadly, most of the participants were children and men. There was little attendance from the women of the community. It seemed to me that this was simply the way of the culture.

I soon joined the chaos and learned the simple rules. The trick was to throw the powder at anyone you encountered and then you were obliged to let him/her respond with his powder weapons. Everyone knew the rules so nobody was upset or offended by the actions.

The fun wasn't limited to just pedestrians. I joined a large group of drummers and other powder fighters waiting for passing cars and motorcyclists to attack. Anyone who arrived at the crossroad dressed in white was fair game. They ended up at the other side of the road covered in purple, yellow, red or green.

After a while, it started to rain and all the colors on my skin merged into one big rainbow of body paint. In the downpour, the streets became a living art gallery with shimmering colors everywhere. The rain poured rivers of color and mud into the streets as we drank rum, played drums and laughed at everything. We partied into the night until we were completely exhausted.

During my stay in Anjuna, I met Leo, a yoga teacher from Argentina and Adam a tourist from Singapore. We shared the road for a while and traveled to Arambol together to roam the hippie villages and explore the bohemian culture of this popular beach town.

In Arambol, yoga, meditation, live music, dance and a variety of healing arts were major attractions to people who came here from all over the world. There were hippie villages on the beach where I could stay for as little as $5US a night and enjoy a stunning ocean view as well. Leo, Adam and I met some amiable people from Denmark, the UK and the States. We hung out together for a while and enjoyed strolling through the markets on the beach that sold everything from beads to food.

Most of my evenings started in the local restaurant where spiritual seekers, artists and other tourists ate. While I enjoyed vegetables topped with delicious Masala sauce, I prepared for the night show in a restaurant, Loeki. I had the opportunity to perform a very old song made famous by Louis Armstrong in 1929, "When You're Smiling", that I had learned to play on my guitar. I was introduced to an amazing instrument called the Hang that had been designed in Switzerland by musicians. Although it looked rather like something you would find in your kitchen, it produced some of the most heavenly and ethereal music I had ever heard.

The underground drug culture of the famous Goa parties attracted many foreigners. I decided to attend one of the gatherings. It was more about satisfying my curiosity than me participating in the drugs that were easily available and that seemed to turn the partiers into disconnected, spaced out people. Occasionally, I had tried marijuana but not being a smoker, it hurt my throat and ultimately made me sleepy and bored.

The local hippies here were amusing to me. They dressed in brilliantly colored oversize garb, were covered in tattoos, wore all manner of accessories and sported the essential hippie dreadlocks. In their pot-induced trances, they pretended to understand the nature of the Universe and all of its secrets.

Opposite to the essence of spiritually awakened people that I admired, these supposed gurus always seemed to be quite serious. They rarely smiled or laughed. Apparently, their profound awareness kept them focused on the more serious side of Divine connection! We silently laughed at their solemn approach. From everything I had learned, a sense of humor and the ability to laugh at yourself was key to a less egoic perspective of life and a more enlightened approach.

AWAKENING INSIGHT

Being spiritual does not mean never laughing or having fun.
Spiritual awakening means developing a healthy sense of humor
and the ability to laugh at yourself in a childlike manner. It is
the way to kill the ego and love yourself at the same time.

Arambol, like all of Goa, is influenced by its Portuguese heritage. I visited some of the churches and explored the architecture with the new companions that Leo, Adam and I had met. One of them, it turned out, was a philosopher and one was a drama writer, which made for interesting conversations and stimulating company.

During my stay in Goa, I spent a great deal of time touring on my moped. I loved swimming in the ocean and reading as many spiritual books as my intuition would find.

I left Goa for Mumbai with a greater tolerance for others and feeling personally stronger and more confident in myself.

230

My touching back into music reminded me that I had talent and potential if I wanted to explore it further. The connections I had experienced with 'metrosexual' hippies (those who were overly attentive to their looks and image) had sparked a great deal of curiosity in me and led me to open more to oriental spirituality. Every day, I was breaking through my old, limiting beliefs.

Leo and I went on to Mumbai while Adam returned to Anjuna.

Mumbai And The Bollywood Debut

Mumbai, formerly known as Bombay, is the largest city in India. Its 20 million people who live in the city proper and outlying districts contribute to the massive throng of pulsating life that takes place within the metropolis. Mumbai is really a miniature representation of India's extremes as it offers everything from the ancient and the spiritual to modern shopping malls and high tech industry and business. The city is a soup of devastating areas of poverty (over half the population inhabits the notorious slums of Mumbai) dotted with areas of equally upscale pockets of incredible wealth.

Situated on the west coast of India with a natural deep-water harbor, it is a center of world commerce and finance that offers a significant contribution to the employment and economy of India.

Its heaving collection of humanity offers everything from insane traffic snarls to ample bars and restaurants to naturopathic science to its own brand of entertainment and fashion.

On one of my first days in Mumbai, someone stopped me on the street corner and asked if I wanted to take part in a movie production as an extra. It sounded like a fun experience so of course I agreed and Leo joined in as well. The next day I was on a broken down bus full of other foreigners from all over the world taking a two hour drive to the movie production center known as Bollywood.

We were given something to eat and costumes to wear. As my role was to be an extra at a cocktail party scene, my outfit was a fake Armani black suit. While waiting to be called to the set, Leo and I walked around the Bollywood complex and visited other movie sites. I pretended to be a professional photographer and was granted permission to freely take pictures of the stars.

We eventually returned to our movie set and got to work. The movie was called Krazzz. It was a love story between a princess named Kamini and a man, Ravi Verma. My part required me to laugh and appear to be having a good time as the princess passed by me at the cocktail party. The director Satish Kaushik kept pushing me to be more passionate about enjoying the party. In an effort to comply, I over acted and forced an outrageously loud laugh, which seemed to be what he was wanting of me. He loved it.

"Very good, this is very good. Keep doing it." He congratulated me and seriously confirmed my great acting skills. I did not know what to say but I burst out with even more laughter at the absurdity of it all. This time it was real.

We were paid the equivalent of $20US and asked to come back the next day. However, most of us were tired of the heat and the acting work. Instead of returning to studio the next day, two Danish women I had met in Goa and I chose to go to the cinema. We took in a four-hour Bollywood movie in an attempt to understand this genre better. It was not the most entertaining movie although it did have colorful dancing and catchy music mixed in with the bad special effects and unimaginative love scenes. After this film, I had had enough of the Bollywood scene and was ready to depart Mumbai for the north of India and more spiritual experiences.

Train Stories

Traveling in India definitely requires patience and tolerance. Because of the bad state of the roads and the long distances between cities, it is preferred to travel by train.

Trains seem to universally create more opportunities for friendships and getting to know fellow passengers. I think about my experiences on the train from Moscow to Beijing and felt that my time on Indian trains was similar. One day I was offered food from a stranger as he taught me to eat it with my hands.

"Would you like to try?" A friendly older lady with a strong Indian accent offered me a share of her food.

"Wow! I did not know that you eat it with your hands. Interesting. I would like to try. Thank you!" I said really surprised as it was in the first month of my Indian trip and I was still adjusting to the country

"Where are you going?" She asked me.

"Up to Northern India or wherever this train will take me!" I said laughing and pointing out that it was a joke.

"India is beautiful. You will enjoy your trip!"

There were interactions with playful children who had a habit of surrounding me and asking silly questions.

"Hello Uncle, are you married?"

"Uncle, uncle, which animal does this and that?"

"Uncle, uncle, why are you traveling alone?"

"Uncle, uncle do you have a girlfriend?"

In one event, the train car I was in was unexpectedly received a visit from a rather imposing, panhandling transvestite. She was dressed in a blue sari and played a flute to a live cobra that danced in front of me.

As I was moving into the northern regions of India from the south, I spent a short while in Ajanta and Ellora. These villages are the site of the magnificent ancient Hindu and Buddhist temples carved in massive caves. The Buddhist caves of Ajanta and the Hindu caves of Ellora were both built by monks in the second century B.C.E. These caves were places of worship, education and the arts and are believed to be, according to the Indian government, the "finest surviving examples of Indian art".

Laughing Yogi

Looking out over Lake Pichola, the fairy tale Lake Palace is one of the most romantic settings in all of India. The Palace built in mid 1700's on the shores of the lake has panoramic views of the city of Udaipur. The beauty of this city has attracted many Hollywood and Bollywood movies to be filmed in its serene setting.

There is a belief that laughter can be a healing modality and is a type of yoga that is practiced in India. In Udaipur I was fortunate to meet a man whom I suspected practiced this type of yoga or at least had developed the lighthearted attitude of the approach. When I happened to ask him for directions, he offered to pose with his wife so I could take a picture of them. His face was so filled with merriment that it completely interrupted my photography.

When I pointed my camera at him, he burst into laughter so contagious that I started laughing so hard I could not even hold the camera steady for the picture. Each time I tried to ask him something he looked at me with his funny face that set me off again and made me forget what I was going to ask. I have never heard anyone in my life whose laugh was quite like that. The sound of it and his facial expression had transformative powers. He made my day and surprisingly, whenever I think of him even today, I feel the same response as if it just happened.

AWAKENING INSIGHT

*Because of a brief meeting with a 'Laughing Yogi'
in Udaipur, I can always tap into the healing
power of laughter with that memory.*

Stone Scam

Jaipur was the next stop along my Indian path. Nestled within arid hills and built on the edge of a lake, Northern India's Jaipur is known as the Pink City and offers a stunning array of temples, palaces and forts for exploring. With a population of over 3 million, Jaipur is a major tourist attraction.

While walking around the desert-like Jaipur I was invited to attend a wedding by some friendly young men I met. We had a nice chat and I took their phone number so I could confirm later. I first wanted to take some pictures of the beautiful city's famous City Palace with its sprawling complex of structures and gardens. I had to climb the tallest building in the area in order to get a rooftop view for my pictures.

At the top of the building, there were shops selling precious stones and jewelry that are traded all over the world. I had read about these and asked one of the shop owners if I could take pictures of his collection of precious stones. He generously gave me permission to do so. We struck up a conversation in which he warned me about mafia people in Jaipur. These criminals scam Europeans into believing that they can start a retail business in Europe by re-selling the fake stones they get them to buy in Jaipur.

"Most tourists cannot differentiate between the real and fake ones and they get trapped in a scam." He explained.

It wasn't twenty minutes after I had been invited to the wedding on the other side of town when I had entered this shop. I looked out onto the street to see these same guys sitting outside the building. I had been telling the shop owner about my wedding invitation and was shocked when he looked out at the motorcyclists and asked if they were the 'wedding guys'. He identified the people as working for the local mafia.

"Thank you for helping me out, sir. I never would have known without meeting you." I said with a sense of deep gratitude for being saved.

In the last two months surrounded by the happy and friendly Indians I had almost forgotten to be careful. I guess it is part of traveler's karma to be exposed to all type of scams.

AWAKENING INSIGHT

Be aware of coincidences. Many times we are unaware of the presence of angels in our lives as the positive spirits that make sure we are safe and who help us avoid trouble. Sometimes it takes a clear mind and body to hear the inner voices and to recognize the presence of these protective spirits.

Exorcism Live

Not far from Jaipur, is a temple called Mehandipur Balaji Mandir. It is considered to be a place for ritualistic healing and exorcisms that attracts many pilgrims to its doors.

I witnessed a live exorcism of a pretty young woman who allegedly was possessed by a demon. She was attached to a wall with chains and her body was shaking uncontrollably. At the same time older women were holding candles and chanting some mysterious songs. The energy of the place was so intense that after few minutes I felt unsafe, completely drained and needed to leave. To me, it was another proof of the existence of dark forces in the invisible world.

AWAKENING INSIGHT
Witnessing exorcisms on a young lady possessed by demons I saw more proof of the existence of dark forces in the invisible world.

The Law Of Attraction In Action

When the weather becomes unbearably hot in India, travelers seeking enlightenment and cool temperatures move north up to the town of McLeod Ganj to the 6,800-foot elevation level in the Himalayas.

McLeod is a village in the Himalayas with a very special energy that attracts all types of spiritual seekers especially in the summer time. It is close to Dharamsala, the official capital in exile of the Tibetan people who escaped persecution from the Chinese in their own country. McLeod Ganj is a small charming and peaceful village with a Buddhist influence that offers many spiritual courses in yoga, meditation, Reiki, reflexology and even instruction about the Mayan Calendar. Many tourists arrive there to study Tibetan Buddhism as well as to learn about the Tibetan culture and crafts.

Local bookstores and small cafes offer for purchase or exchange practically any book that has ever been published about spiritual topics. It is a paradise for travelers looking for the deeper meaning in life.

Since I had watched "The Secret" for the first time in London in 2007, I had been looking for signs to prove The Law of Attraction worked in everyday life. I also wanted to learn how to apply it in my own life.

Initially I visited McLeod Ganj to participate in their ten-day course entitled "Introduction to Buddhism". I was ready for a change of pace after months of beach bumming, partying and temple sightseeing. My goal was also to find an ashram and learn yoga and meditation but this course was as close as I could come. After visiting the Buddhist Center where the classes would be held, I decided to give it a try. I signed up for the course, which was to start in few weeks.

To kill time, I took some random yoga classes with a young teacher named Krishna. I liked his sessions but soon found Agama Yoga School on the other side of town, which was recommended by my friend, Leo when we were together in Mumbai. I took the first free class to find out if it suited my needs.

The course was led by Manu from Belgium and Monica born in India but raised in U.S. The very first yoga posture we practised, the spinal twist, was the one which coincidentally caused me the most pain in my hips due to my natural lack of flexibility there. It was as if this class was perfectly crafted for my health requirements. I also attended Monica's evening classes which were about understanding, controlling and managing dreams. It was another small coincidence since I had recently been having strange dreams that I did not understand.

It seemed that Agama Yoga was a good fit and a helpful way to pass the time before the Buddhism classes. I decided to move my accommodation closer to the Yoga Center. I checked in to my new room only to realize that my roommate was Krishna, my first yoga teacher in McLeod. It turned out that he had been a graphic designer as well so we had plenty to talk about.

As we talked, our conversation turned to the subject of coincidences, which I had been noticing a lot of lately. He recommended that I watch a movie called "What the Bleep Do We Know?" It dealt with this subject and many more topics that were important, burning questions to me. When I watched the film, I could not beliee what I saw. Not only did this movie address the very same information that was in "The Secret", but it did it in a way that was a bit more scientific and informative which appealed to me.

The movie was based on a series of interviews with scientists and experts in the field of psychology, quantum physicists, and spirituality who explain the phenomenon of quantum physics and how it relates to our thoughts and how our thoughts in turn affect the outcomes of our lives. It was supported by a fictional story about a woman who discovers how to transform her unhappy life through tapping into the power of her own thoughts. Japanese scientist, Dr. Massaru Emoto demonstrated how water crystals take on the energy of the surroundings. It was a graphic illustration of how our thoughts impact our physical environment.

Every minute I watched the movie, the more and more fascinating it became to me. In fact, I had to pause occasionally to simply take a deep breath, leave the room and stare at the mountain peaks, admire birds and enjoy the refreshing breezes from the Himalayan wind.

As I had always done in my life, I asked God for a sign that this was truth. I took few deep pranayama breaths and came back with a fresh and open mind to my room to continue watching the movie. A minute later I realized that the main character in the story was a photographer who was going to a Polish wedding to take pictures. Another coincidence? How many American movies use the subject of a Polish wedding? But the truly astounding part that got my attention was who was getting married? *Filip-owski* and Humansky. Now, why would a script writer choose those strange names? It was a clear message for me that was the answer to my prayer. It was the sign I needed to affirm that The Law of Attraction works. Ask and it will always be given.

AWAKENING INSIGHT
Through the synchronicity of various events, it is possible to discover the answers to any question you have. It requires focus and paying attention to what happens in your life but the answer will be there. Ask and it will be given.

From that moment, I started to visualize outcomes that I desired. The results were astounding. People I wanted to pay attention to me began to be more friendly; I became attractive to a beautiful woman who had previously not even noticed me; even the primping and narcissistic 'metrosexual' hippies asked me to play guitar with them; I was also miraculously able to mentally control flies and mosquitos to leave me alone when I was meditating.

These experiences were real proof that there is a force in the Universe that is responsible for the entire life experience on Earth. I now understood that all questions if asked with care and precision are answered either through meditation, dream, inner voice or a series of synchronistic events.

We all have the potential to be super human beings, to be enlightened, to live our own 'heaven on Earth', to be like Jesus, Buddha, or any highly evolved spiritual being. All we have to do is ask how to peel away the dull stone layer to reveal the diamond underneath. When we ask, we simply have to listen to the inner voice that will give us guidance.

AWAKENING INSIGHT

The answers to all questions and the fulfillment of our desires lie in the powerful potential of our spiritual being-ness. We can be like Buddha, Jesus or any highly evolved being. When we ask very precisely for what we want, our inner voice will offer guidance through meditation, dream or synchronistic events.

The day finally arrived to begin the " Introduction to Buddhism" course. It was just a twenty-minute walk to move from where I was staying with Krishna to the Tushita Meditation Center – just far enough to be able to enjoy the complete silence and be inspired by the beauty of the Himalayas and the wildlife that lived there.

The course was designed to instruct participants in the Buddha's teachings and to explain the steps of meditation based on Mahayana Buddhist philosophy. Initially I only wanted to learn about the basics of Buddhism so I could compare it to my Christian beliefs. I soon discovered, however, that it was a great way to detoxify from the whole outside world in which I had been so intensely immersed.

At the Center, I shared a room with two friendly American students but we were not allowed to talk to each other. Each day we woke up early for meditation, ate breakfast, and then worked as volunteers in the ashram. In my case, I washed dishes. After our chores were completed, we attended a Buddha teaching class. During the instruction, I learned how to meditate by focusing on my breath. Doing so sharpened my mind and cleared my thoughts. There were also guided meditations that allowed us to get a deeper understanding of Buddhism principles. After the class, there was more meditation, which sometimes was a walking meditation.

On one of these contemplative exercises, I spotted a wild bear grazing nearby and was always aware of the monkeys jumping on the roof when we meditated indoors. The close interactions with nature added a mystical dimension to the whole experience. Our teacher, a British woman who was also a monk often talked of the monkeys who interrupted our quiet meditations as the great patience teachers. I loved that expression.

The meditations were followed by a one-hour group exercise. This was the only time we were allowed to speak.

For the first time in my life I got the concept of unity, kindness, love and compassion for all sentient beings. I grasped the idea of love as a sincere wish for others to be happy.

AWAKENING INSIGHT
Love is a sincere wish for others to be happy.

I finally understood the wisdom in the Buddha's teachings, which were similar to those of Jesus' principles. The Buddha's lessons used different terminology and were more based on logic than faith but I found I could easily love both of these approaches.

AWAKENING INSIGHT
The Buddha's teachings are similar in principle to those of Jesus. The difference is in how it is expressed. Buddhism is based more on logic than faith but both approaches were compatible.

We also learned a lot about karma. By understanding the law of karma in our lives, I could see that reincarnation might be the only reasonable explanation for the injustices in the world. I had always wondered why bad things happen to good people and how it was that seemingly bad people often had little adversity in their lives. It was very different from the Christian concept I had grown up with but it made complete sense to me and answered many questions that had been with me since childhood.

AWAKENING INSIGHT
By studying law of karma I saw reincarnation as the only reasonable explanation of the injustices and inequalities of the world.

I also became familiar with the idea of "the monkey mind" which was the name given to the racing thoughts that seem to invade our consciousness in a running commentary about our lives. From the Buddhist perspective, this is a constant source of unhappiness and suffering.

STATISTIC
Scientific research claims that the human brain produces approximately 60,000 thoughts a day, from which about 70-80 percent are negative and repetitive.

We suffer because our mind is polluted by attachment, ego, anger, or distorted views of the nature of reality. Our happiness can be accessed as a natural result of having a healthy, clear mind.

AWAKENING INSIGHT
According to Buddha, the untrained mind also called "The Monkey Mind" is a source of all unhappiness and suffering.

During the group meetings where we were able to freely express, I was surprised to discover that I was the only one in the group who considered himself to be a happy person. The other western, wealthier travelers seemed to have some form of suffering in their lives. This realization gave me a sense of being above them and, unfortunately, at that time, I had little compassion for their situations. Somewhere deep inside, I realized that my reactions were coming from my cultural sense of feeling inferior. I recognized my subconscious anger at having to fight to get what they had. I became aware of my suppressed envy that they had been handed everything from birth.

Even so, I felt good about myself knowing that I was seen as the only one having succeeded where others had not. I also felt like my personal struggles had made me strong and able to meet life's challenges and make my life the happy experience that it was.

However, I didn't realize that the happiness I was feeling did not come from my own inner peace, which is the source of genuine happiness. Instead, I was looking outside myself and believing my interesting and adventurous life was the reason I was happy. More of that realization was in my future.

AWAKENING INSIGHT
Most of our daily thoughts are repetitive and negative. These thoughts shape our destiny on daily basis. To live a happy life it is crucial to detach from thoughts by practicing living in now.

I learned that, in order to have a healthy mind one needed to break the old habits of painful, negative thinking. Practicing meditation and living in the present moment as Eckhart Tolle teaches, is the way to change those old patterns that keep us from being joyful in life. In his work, Tolle quotes both Buddha and Jesus many times, which expanded my prior limited beliefs about religion.

AWAKENING INSIGHT
Happiness can be reached as a natural result of having a healthy, clear mind. Practicing meditation is the key to that clarity.

Many spiritual traditions state that thoughts create reality and our outer world is nothing more than a reflection of our inner world. Through my time in McLeod Ganj I discovered what a powerful tool meditation is and how vital it is in creating the outer world we desire.

AWAKENING INSIGHT
Thoughts create reality and the outer world is nothing more than a reflection of the inner world.

India was the first country on the road where I had deep spiritual experiences. In McLeod Ganj especially, I was opened up and saw my own Divine nature. I was given the gift of observing life through the lens of spirituality that was not necessarily religiously focused. I understood that my world journey had begun partly as my personal search for this knowledge. Thailand had been an awakening through wounding for me. In India, I began the process of change and transformation in my life and I now had some tools to continue the journey.

AWAKENING INSIGHT

*Meditation, yoga and visualisations are essential tools
for well being. These techniques enable growth, more
focused goals and greater enjoyment in life.*

A big part of the support for me were the books I read. They helped clarify many doubts and answered my questions about the meaning of life.

RECOMMENDED BOOKS

I strongly recommend reading such works as:

> *"The Power of Now" and "A New Earth" by Eckhart Tolle;*
> *"Jesus Lived in India" by Holger Kersaten;*
> *"Personal Development" by Swami Mumukshananda;*
> *"Surrender to Existence" by Osho;*
> *"The Law of Attraction" by Michael Losier;*
> *"Love and Compassion" by Dalai Lama.*

I even read "The God Delusion" by Richard Dawkins to gain a broader perspective of spirituality. Although I respect his statements I believe that life cannot be explained with just our five basic senses. We have to take into account our intuition and the creativity and knowingness of our right brain.

The power of the invisible forces of the Universe were quickly becoming a deep seated conviction within me and reading all these books only strengthened my trust. The writings opened my life to new possibilities and helped me understand how to live a better, stronger, more passionate existence.

AWAKENING INSIGHT

*Spiritual books expand consciousness and help in understanding
how to live a better, stronger, more passionate life.*

I will be forever grateful for the good fortune I had in meeting a British woman in McLeod Ganj when I first arrived. In the few days we spent together chatting and touring the town, she was the one who found the course and encouraged me to check out the Tushita Meditation Center. After the class ended, I spent a few blessed days being with other spiritual seekers and enjoying my new happiness. I left there feeling renewed and absolutely not the same person who arrived.

I continued my northern India adventures in Agra, the home of the Taj Majal, which was my next stop.

The Price Paid For Sightseeing

The city of Agra is a major administrative district in Uttar Pradesh and a prime tourist destination due to its historic ancient structures such as the Taj Mahal.

The day before visiting Taj Mahal, I explored the ruins of Fort Amar Singh Gate. This area, which is really a walled city, was the site of a battle that marked the takeover of India by the British in modern history. Its architecture is a rich mixture of both Islamic and Hindu influences.

A young man offered himself as my guide. He said he would do it for free as he wanted to practice his English. I cautiously agreed having been burned before in such matters. Not surprisingly, at the end of our tour, he asked for money. I refused to pay him because we had not agreed to it. He became annoying and started begging me for money. My response was to quickly walk away towards exit of the Fort.

As I was leaving, I heard him shout something in Hindi and suddenly hundreds of bees swarmed around me. I remembered all the painful bites from my childhood. The more I panicked and tried to run away, the more they came after me. Somebody from the nearby crowd advised me not to move my hands since white attracts bees and I was wearing a white Indian shirt.

In the midst of the chaos, I used the same prayer as I had with the stray dogs in Bali. I asked God for help. As I started to pray, I calmed down and after a while the bees left me alone. I was very lucky not to be bitten but after this stressful situation I was not in the mood to do anything. I went back home and watched two Woody Allen movies from the complete collection that I had bought in Thailand.

AWAKENING INSIGHT
*There are some people in the world who know how
to use forces of nature for dark purposes.*

The next day, having recovered from the bee-swarming incident, I went out to visit Taj Majal, by many considered the most beautiful structure in the world. It is strange but seeing such extreme poverty on the streets of Agra and knowing how much it cost to build this structure I had real difficulty enjoying the beauty of it even if it was a Wonder of the World. I took some pictures, walked in the building and rather unimpressed, came back home.

The legend says that the structure was built as a memorial to the king's beloved wife who died in childbirth. Apparently he was so heartbroken at her death that his hair turned completely white overnight! The construction of the complex is said to have taken over twenty years to complete.

Despite this touching information, it was hard for me to feel attachment to the beauty of the edifice when so much suffering seemed to be a part of it currently. On the other hand, I had to admit that the motives were definitely from the heart of love, which is part of what was built into it as well.

Staying With Locals

While waiting for my train to arrive at the Agra railway station, I picked up my guitar and started playing. In a very short time, I had attracted a huge crowd of passionate fans listening to me closely and looking at me with admiration. I finished my song to the applause of the crowd, feeling more appreciated than I ever had in my short music career. I might as well have been one of the Beatles. When the train arrived I jumped onboard and bid my admirers goodbye.

On the train to Amritsar, I made the acquaintance of an Indian man named Robert. He introduced himself to me and we shared a pleasant conversation and new friendship. "Hello my name is Robert. Where are you from?" Asked an elegant forty something man.

"From Poland, and you?" I asked laughing since it was very obvious he was Indian.

"I am from India!" He answered seriously not understanding my joke.

"Nice to meet you then."

"Nice to met you too."

"Where are you going?" Indian people love to ask questions.

"I am going to Amritsar."

"Come with me, I am living in Amritsar. You can stay with my family. I will show you an Indian Pakistani border ceremony. You will like it." He seemed very welcoming and I felt that I could trust him.

"Ok, sounds good to me." I replied.

"You should be traveling in the first class. Hold on a second..." He called the train manager and explained to him that I should be moved to first class.

Robert was coming back from a month long spiritual retreat and apparently decided to invite a stranger to his house. He may also have seen me playing my guitar and thought I was a real rock star. Whatever his motives, I was grateful for his offer.

When we arrived in Amritsar, he showed me my room and introduced me to his five-year old son, who was very friendly and funny. From my perspective, Robert turned out to be rather serious although helpful. He treated his wife as if she was hired help rather than his spouse, which I found a bit disturbing. I assumed it was simply the Indian culture.

The next day, the three of us went to see the promised Pakistani/Indian ceremony. It took place in a village called, Wagah, on the Pakistan/Indian border. What I was about to see was a daily ritual that commemorated the division of this town between Pakistan and India in the 1947 independence of India from Britain. Michael Palin, travel documentary filmmaker and former member of the Month Python comedy group, labeled this ceremony as a perfect display of "controlled contempt".

It was so precisely choreographed that it appeared to be well acted. In fact it was all very real and very serious to the players although it struck me as having its humorous moments. The soldiers with their big mustaches and puffed out chests turned upwards to the sky came from each side of the border. They marched, Monty Python's "Ministry of Funny Walks" style towards each other to the center of the town where there was a closed border gate.

At sunset, the gates were opened and each side lowered their respective flags simultaneously. The whole display ended with the flags being folded, a brisk handshake exchanged between sides, the gate closed and the soldiers from both sides retreating from the border.

I found it hard to take the ceremony seriously especially considering the applauding and cheering crowd who were apparently fully enjoying the spectacle. We laughed and I took some pictures and we went back home. It was a strange day!

The next day I visited the Golden Temple of Amritsar. It was a stunning spectacle to see this beautiful temple's shimmering gold exterior reflecting the light of the day. I was amazed to learn that the temple, which was built by Sikhs in the 1600's, was designed as a place that would be open to men and women from all walks of life.

The shrine has four entrances from all four directions signifying a welcome to all who visit. Even today it still is a spiritual gathering place for people of all religions. I was astounded to learn that over 100,000 visit this temple daily to pray and worship.

After having had the privilege of experiencing the Golden Temple, I was ready to leave. In return for Robert's hospitality, I had promised to send him pictures of his son that I had taken. However, as much as I wanted to thank him for his kindness, I lost his information and thus can only send energetic gratitude to him and hope that life will pay him back.

Holy River

It was already June, one of the hottest months in India. I decided to visit the sacred and boiling hot Varanasi, an ancient city on the Ganges River in Northeastern India.

This holy city is considered to be one of the spiritual capitals of India. Famous for its body cremation ceremonies on the Ganges, its magical temples and architecture as well as its attraction to tourists for religious reasons, left no shortage of new experiences to absorb.

I saw the process of burning the bodies and throwing them into the river. Some say that in order to avoid skeletons rising to the surface, they attach a stone to each corpse to weigh them down. Sometimes the stones come loose and the remains can surface anywhere including right between children playing in the river and their parents taking a bath. Most shocking to me was the fact that nobody makes a big deal about it.

~

India was by far the strangest and the most inspiring and challenging country I visited. After my extended stay, I understood why many call it "the spiritual capital of the world" and why others complain about its "dirtiness and chaos".

India – love it or hate it.

Indeed it can be dirty, smelly, shocking and full of contrasts. In one day one can find peace and stress, spirituality and superficiality, arranged marriages and romantic Bollywood stories, money obsessed gurus and humble bus riding teachers.

This might explain why India is a favorite place for seekers from all walks of life. Although it has a lot of poverty, it is still safe for travelers. Before going to Nepal I left my wallet in a restaurant. It took me about a half an hour to realize my loss. When I came back I found it untouched with all the money inside.

As my three-month visa was expiring, I was ready to move to the last country on my Asian continent itinerary. I was on my way to Nepal and to take in the beauty and mystique of the Himalayas.

Nepal
"Five elements, Everest Base Camp Trek"

Nepal, Kathmandu, Mount Everest

Mount Everest

Kathmandu, the capital city of Nepal, has it is own specific mountain charm, but the best parts of the country are its two famous treks in the Himalayas: Annapurna and the Mount Everest Base Camp journey. Both are visually stunning and famous for their amazing mountains, inspiring Buddhist temples and high river bridges that hang over mountain rapids.

I chose the Mount Everest Base Camp trek, which takes about twelve days there and back. I elected to go on my own as most backpackers did but of course, along the way, there were plenty of Sherpa people available who were transporting equipment for other groups.

I soon found myself on a small plane from Kathmandu to Lukla Airport, considered to be one of the most dangerous airports in the world. I was flying with one other tourist, a flight attendant, the pilot and many bags of rice.

Once we landed I immediately began the journey. After an hour I stopped at one of the Sherpa houses and shared an alcoholic drink and some food with a few of them.

"Hello, can I see the menu?" I asked a young girl who was working in this home-made restaurant.

"Here you are!" She said and joined the other young Sherpas in the conversation. They were drinking some white liquid that looked like milk but seeing them be very enthusiastic, I was sure it was some type of alcoholic drink.

"Excuse me, what is that? Can I try it?" I asked curious.

"Sure, here you are!" They said in friendly broken English.

"You guys work as porters, am I right?" I had seen them carrying big bags belonging to tourists.

"Yes we do! Sit down with us!" They were laughing and motioned to me to join them.

They were very young and did not speak much English but we managed to communicate very well despite the language barrier.

I continued on my walk even though I was feeling a bit dizzy from the altitude and the drink. I don't know why but I decided to drink water directly from the river. I guess I naively thought that if it was in the Himalayas, it must be clean. About an hour later, I started feeling pain in my stomach that caused me to look for a place to sleep so I could recover.

The next day I felt better and continued making my way past stunning views. I visited charming villages and amazing red Buddhist temples where I tried to meditate with the local monks. Their process and chanting were difficult for me to follow especially since I hadn't meditated since leaving McLeod Ganj but I was able to stay with it for a short time.

On the way I met other fellow travelers from Israel, Australia and Canada. We hung out together for a while but then had to split up due to our different resistances to the altitude, which required staying at certain levels for extended periods of time in order to acclimatize to the thinner atmosphere.

I learned a lot from the people I met on this journey. An Israeli couple taught me about tolerance. From Australians I clarified the principles of Buddhism. A Canadian guy showed me how to be strong. They all were great teachers, but I learned the most from the silent mountains. During these days I understood how difficult it was to stay present and to put all the theory I had learned into practice. This was the ultimate challenge.

Thousand of thoughts were running through my mind. I was jumping between past events and future possibilities. Despite being tired and dizzy, having a headache from the altitude and my constant stomach pain, I finally reached the final peak at 18,000 feet.

The air was crisp and fresh. The view was spectacular with hundreds of prayer flags planted nearby that were waving in the wind. I watched the five colors of flags that represent different elements: ether, air, fire, water and earth. According to Tibetan tradition, health and harmony can be reached through the balance of these five elements.

As I sat at the top of the planned summit and enjoyed the view in silence, I finally realized the big picture and the significance of the immense effort I had put out during my trek. I was overcome with a sensation of deep peace and harmony that spontaneously flowed through me. It was a moment of that unity, love and compassion that I had learned at McLeod Ganj and it was a feeling of deep love for myself and for all sentient beings in that moment. After appreciating this glorious moment, I was ready to come back to Kathmandu.

AWAKENING INSIGHT
You can find human teachers everywhere but the
most powerful guide is in the silence of nature.
Balancing the elements of ether, air, fire, water and earth
in the Tibetan tradition leads to health and harmony.

On the way back to Kathmandu from Lukla, I exchanged t-shirts with a Tibetan man. I gave him my green T-shirt with Rajnikanth, an Indian Arnold Schwarzenegger character, who I joked with him, was my uncle. In exchange, he gave me a black t-shirt with Britney Spears dressed as a Hindu goddess on it.

Later on when I wore this shirt in various parts of the world, it was a great way to tell the story and make friends among backpackers. The only place it didn't attract attention was in Manhattan where nobody really seemed to care.

Losing Faith In Local People

When I came back to Kathmandu, I downloaded all my pictures to my hard-drive and left it in hotel. The same day I bought a one-way ticket to New York, a USA "Lonely Planet Guide", and filters for my camera. Happy, excited and satisfied, I walked around in the city with a big smile on my face.

I saw tourists drinking coffee in Starbucks and eating burgers in McDonald's. This had never been my type of traveling. It was hard for me to understand why westerners would travel to a foreign country only to do the same things they do at home.

My philosophy of travel was simple - make local friends and learn from them by trying to live their lifestyle. Sometime the interactions where painful, but I guess everyone has different lessons to learn. My lesson was to be learned in Kathmandu.

In order to avoid the western type cafes, I walked around and found a family run, small restaurant full of peaceful people. As Nepal has a reputation for being one of the friendliest countries in Asia, I was feeling safe and at ease. I sat down at the big wooden table, asked for a coffee, opened my brand new book and started reading. I put my camera in my bag and held it between my knees.

I asked for another coffee and after about an hour, I noticed my neck started to itch. The more I scratched it, the itchier it became. It felt as if a hundred mosquitos had bitten me in the same spot. I could not figure out where this had come from. I looked up at the ceiling to see if maybe something had dropped onto me but did not see anything. It got so uncomfortable that I asked for water.

Suddenly a man from the crowd, dressed in a white shirt asked me what happened. When I told him, he said it must have been mosquito bite. I ignored him and asked the lady from the restaurant to bring a jar of water. At this point, I didn't realize that someone had put a substance on my neck to cause the itching. It was part of the robbery deception.

I put my bag on the chair next to me, stood up and let the lady pour the water on my neck. It lasted only a second or two. When I straightened up, the bag with my camera was gone. I started to scream, which caused everyone to look at me in surprise. They all acted like they did not see what had happened. The man in the white shirt said he saw a small guy running away with my bag.

I paid twenty dollars up front to one of the observers to help me find my camera. We looked everywhere for the thief including checking out camera shops, police stations and areas of the city that were very dodgy but never found the camera. It was gone forever. It reminded me that I trusted people too much and I was paying the price.

"Maybe the gringos were right to drink their coffee at Starbucks." I thought sadly. I was devastated by this turn of events that left me angry with myself and disappointed in the people I had thought I could trust.

The next day I was on the plane to the U.S., happy to come back to the normal world. I was eager and curious about the next segment of my adventures and the inspiring stories waiting to unfold in the West.

"Who am I?"

"What do I want?"

PART V

REFLECTIONS SO FAR AND LOOKING AHEAD

While taking the long flight from Kathmandu to New York I had time to consider all the lessons and experiences I had gained on the road so far. I imagined teleporting back in time and talking to a younger version of myself.

I wondered what that young 'me' who had pinned the places on a map in his bedroom in Poland would say to the 'me' flying to America to continue his world journey.

Would he be surprised at some of the experiences that had happened? Would he be wide-eyed with admiration at all that I had encountered? What would he think about the spectacular sites I had visited? Would he be amazed that I had done everything and more that he dreamed about back then?

There was a lot I could share with him.

I would tell him how being born with an adventurous spirit, and a strong will was a good thing. That my education and hard work habits although they had sometimes been a struggle at his age, allowed me to have this amazing life adventure. I would tell him how grateful I was for the inner resources that had been developed early in my life because they had supported me on my journey.

I was almost sure that he would be overjoyed to hear how my perspectives about God had changed. They had been such a troubling concern for him back then and had matured into a certainty of God's powerful presence and a deep knowing that my prayers to Him were always answered. My awareness and concepts of God now extended far beyond the boundaries of the Bible that he had questioned so many years earlier. I imagined him listening to my stories about the starry night near Uluru in Australia or the beauty of night swims in the ocean that glowed blue and sparkled from the reflection of the moon or the sacred sunrises I saw that peeked over a volcano. He would hear just how it felt to be so connected to everything in those moments.

As I remembered him, I was sure he would be intrigued and captivated by my experiences and awareness of unseen forces?

I would tell him about the synchronicities and coincidences of chance meetings and guiding conversations that introduced me to books and places that led to discoveries. He would love to see the movie, "What the Bleep Do We Know" and its fascinating revelations. He would laugh at my reactions to being chased by bees at Taj Mahal and he might shrink back at my scary experiences of dark forces in Indonesia.

He would be happy to know that his optimism and enthusiasm were an important part of life that allowed me to keep going. He would be proud to know that I had rarely given up or lost hope. I would confirm for him that truly, I had discovered anything is possible. I would tell him about how being flexible and going with the flow meant so much to me.

And what was most important, I would tell him how much I had changed because of my travels

As I sat at 30,000 feet above the ocean, I knew all these things I would tell him were not in the books I read or the videos I saw but were in the real live experiences I had encountered. To be sure, I was not the same person who had stepped onto Italian soil and fell in love with the beauty of Pisa, Florence and Venice. So much had happened in the past year that it was hard to imagine I had covered that much territory. Flashes of my journeys passed through my thoughts in rapid succession - the spectacular sites of temples and holy places, of expansive underwater magical gardens, of illness and bed bugs, of onsite history lessons and the present moment happiness of watching Buddhist monks and children at play.

There were elephant rides, surfing lessons, meditation and yoga practices, lessons about Chakras and the Law of Attraction. I dated women from exotic countries. I had lived with locals, driven a moped, attended local house parties in Tokyo and slept in a capsule hotel there. I explored the ancient temples of Angkor Wat and the Great Wall of China. There were Full Moon festivals in Thailand, diving in the Philippines, the beauty of India and the evil ceremonies too. And then, there had been my grand finale of a trek in the Himalayas.

I met many new backpacker friends and felt very connected to the cultures and people in all the countries I visited. I knew some of these people would be life-long connections and some were just fleeting angels or devils in my path for my learning and direction. Every encounter was unique and I had tried to be as engaged as possible with each one no matter how long or short it was.

No matter what, nothing was more life giving to me than exchanges of the heart that helped me find out about someone else's life and experiences while I shared mine. For me, it mattered that I could connect openly and honestly with others even if sometimes things didn't work out in my favor. Life was never about holding back. Life was to be lived full on with openness, honesty and passion.

I had certainly run headlong into challenging moments. I had had my possessions stolen. I had been duped in scams and had encountered some shocking events especially in Thailand. In my honesty and naivety I learned that women whom I thought were interested in some form of connection with me were only after my wallet.

Apart of the all the amazing experiences on the road the most rewarding was the fact that I was finally moved and shifted in India. I smiled as I remembered my rainbow paint covered body in the rain at the Holi Festival and my delight at the colorful saris worn by Indian women, the ancient spiritual traditions and energy that blended with the crazy chaotic commerce of places like Mumbai. I remembered the moment of that deep sense of unity, love and compassion for myself and for all sentient beings that had swept over me at the McLeod Ganj retreat. It had powerfully shifted my perception of love in that moment.

Still, I was fully aware that I by no means had resolved all my questions about life's meaning and especially about love and what I was ultimately looking for. Somehow I still struggled with women and my emotional connection to them. I had a feeling that I had not yet understand the deeper motivation and spirituality in the love that I was seeking. Something in me sensed that there were more life changing experiences and true love waiting for me in the Americas where I was headed.

I remembered the wise words of my uncle's magician friend, Janus when I asked him what were his most important life lessons. His reply was exactly what I had been doing in the past year: *follow your own path and do what you love.* It proved to me that there is significance in the people we meet on our life journey and how they can illuminate our choices.

Following advices of Janus my own life path was always about seeking the truth and finding out what was meaningful. From the age of twelve, I knew I wanted to step onto the bigger stage of the world I lived in and I now proudly was aware that I had accomplished that desire. The road was my true passion and somehow I knew I was going in the right direction.

Ahead lay further life lessons that would shatter some of the self-satisfaction I was enjoying at the moment. As much as I felt I had grown and changed, I did not know at that time that my true transformation and profound discoveries lay ahead.

While being open to what was next, I was feeling extreme gratitude for my accomplishments to date. I fell asleep to the drone of aircraft engines that were carrying me toward the next phase of my life.

An American Great Spirit was about to come...another book's worth of adventures lay ahead.

~